Treating Impulse Control Diso

Treating Impulse Control Disorders: A Cognitive-Behavioral Therapy Program

Therapist Guide

Jon E. Grant • Christopher B. Donahue • Brian L. Odlaug

OXFORD
UNIVERSITY PRESS

OXFORD

UNIVERSITY PRESS

Oxford University Press, Inc., publishes works that further
Oxford University's objective of excellence
in research, scholarship, and education.

Oxford   New York
Auckland   Cape Town   Dar es Salaam   Hong Kong   Karachi
Kuala Lumpur   Madrid   Melbourne   Mexico City   Nairobi
New Delhi   Shanghai   Taipei   Toronto

With offices in
Argentina   Austria   Brazil   Chile   Czech Republic   France   Greece
Guatemala   Hungary   Italy   Japan   Poland   Portugal   Singapore
South Korea   Switzerland   Thailand   Turkey   Ukraine   Vietnam

Copyright © 2011 by Oxford University Press, Inc.

Published by Oxford University Press, Inc.
198 Madison Avenue, New York, New York 10016

www.oup.com

Oxford is a registered trademark of Oxford University Press

Library of Congress Cataloging-in-Publication Data
Grant, Jon E.
  Treating impulse control disorders : a cognitive-behavioral therapy program:
therapist guide / Jon E. Grant, Christopher B. Donahue, Brian L. Odlaug.
      p. ; cm.
  Includes bibliographical references.
  ISBN 978-0-19-973879-3 (paper : alk. paper)
  1. Impulse control disorders—Treatment. 2. Cognitive therapy.
I. Donahue, Christopher B. II. Odlaug, Brian L. III. Title.
  [DNLM: 1. Impulse Control Disorders—psychology. 2. Impulse Control
Disorders—therapy. 3. Cognitive Therapy—methods. 4. Self Care. WM 190]
  RC569.5.I46G74 2011
  616.89'1425--dc22
                                                    2010046121

9 8 7 6 5 4 3 2 1

Printed in the United States of America
on acid-free paper

About Treatments *ThatWork*™

Stunning developments in healthcare have taken place over the last several years, but many of our widely accepted interventions and strategies in mental health and behavioral medicine have been brought into question by research evidence as not only lacking benefit, but perhaps inducing harm. Other strategies have been proven effective using the best current standards of evidence, resulting in broad-based recommendations to make these practices more available to the public. Several recent developments are behind this revolution. First, we have arrived at a much deeper understanding of pathology, both psychological and physical, which has led to the development of new, more precisely targeted interventions. Second, our research methodologies have improved substantially, such that we have reduced threats to internal and external validity, making the outcomes more directly applicable to clinical situations. Third, governments around the world, and healthcare systems and policymakers, have decided that the quality of care should improve, that it should be evidence based, and that it is in the public's interest to ensure that this happens (Barlow, 2004; Institute of Medicine, 2001).

Of course, the major stumbling block for clinicians everywhere is the accessibility of newly developed evidence-based psychological interventions. Workshops and books can go only so far in acquainting responsible and conscientious practitioners with the latest behavioral healthcare practices and their applicability to individual patients. This new series, Treatments *ThatWork*™, is devoted to communicating these exciting new interventions to clinicians on the frontlines of practice.

The manuals and workbooks in this series contain step-by-step, detailed procedures for assessing and treating specific problems and diagnoses. But this series also goes beyond the books and manuals by providing ancillary materials that will approximate the supervisory process in assisting practitioners in the implementation of these procedures in their practice.

In our emerging healthcare system, the growing consensus is that evidence-based practice offers the most responsible course of action for the mental health professional. All behavioral healthcare clinicians deeply desire to provide the best possible care for their patients. In this series, our aim is to close the dissemination and information gap and make that possible.

This therapist guide outlines a cognitive-behavioral therapy program for impulse control disorders (CBT-ICD). The program was developed for the treatment of pathological gambling (PG), kleptomania (KM), compulsive buying (CB), and pyromania (PY), and is based on well-established CBT principles that have been proven successful in treating compulsive gamblers.

Therapy is composed of six sessions, with the option of an additional family session. A unique element of this treatment is the use of cue exposure therapy (CET), along with motivational interviewing and behavioral interventions. Clients are taught to recognize those situations or events that trigger their impulses, and then are exposed to their triggers (either in vivo or imaginally) so they can practice managing them without engaging in impulsive behavior. Clients are also taught ways of correcting their erroneous beliefs about their behaviors, as well as strategies for relapse prevention. Home practice and daily self-monitoring are essential to success, and a corresponding workbook contains all the forms and worksheets clients need to complete all in-session and at-home assignments.

CBT-ICD is a time-limited treatment that aims to help individuals with ICDs to understand all the facets of their problem, in order to gain control over their behavior.

David H. Barlow, Editor-in-Chief,
Treatments *ThatWork*™
Boston, MA

References

Barlow, D.H. (2004). Psychological treatments. *American Psychologist, 59,* 869–878.

Institute of Medicine. (2001). *Crossing the quality chasm: A new health system for the 21st century.* Washington, DC: National Academy Press.

Acknowledgments

The authors wish to thank Robert Ladouceur, Nancy Petry, and Matt Kushner, all of whom provided invaluable guidance during the early development of this manualized treatment. Robert Ladouceur also generously allowed us to expand upon aspects of his earlier treatment manual for pathological gambling and apply them to other impulse control disorders.

Table of Contents

Chapter 1 | *Introductory Information for Therapists*

(Corresponds to Chapter 1 of the workbook)

The cognitive-behavioral therapy program for impulse control disorders (CBT-ICD) was developed for the treatment of pathological gambling (PG), kleptomania (KM), compulsive buying (CB), and pyromania (PY). In the introduction, we will review background and diagnostic information for each ICD, as well as available treatment outcome studies. The assessment process for each ICD problem and the individual therapy sessions will be reviewed. Certain treatment materials will differ by the individual ICD, which will be outlined in each therapy session. We believe the CBT-ICD treatment materials will allow clinicians the flexibility to treat one or more ICD problems.

Background Information

Formal impulse control disorders (ICDs) include PG, KM, trichotillomania (TTM), intermittent explosive disorder (IED), and pyromania (PY), and are characterized by difficulties in resisting urges to engage in behaviors that are excessive and/or ultimately harmful to oneself or others (American Psychiatric Association, 2000). Diagnostic criteria have also been proposed for other disorders categorized as ICDs not otherwise specified (NOS) in the *Diagnostic and Statistical Manual of Mental Disorders* (*American Psychiatric Association DSM-IV-TR, 2000*): pathologic skin picking, compulsive sexual behavior (CSB), and compulsive buying (CB). ICDs are relatively common among adolescents and adults, carry significant morbidity and mortality, and can be effectively treated with behavioral and pharmacological therapies. Although the extent to which the ICDs share clinical, genetic, phenomenological, and biological features is incompletely understood, many of the ICDs share the following common core qualities:

1. Repetitive or compulsive engagement in a behavior despite adverse consequences;

2. Diminished control over the problematic behavior;

3. An appetitive urge or craving state prior to engagement in the problematic behavior; and

4. A hedonic quality during the performance of the problematic behavior.

These features have led to a description of ICDs as *behavioral addictions* (Holden, 2001). We will define each ICD problem addressed in this CBT manual and provide current treatment outcome research findings.

Diagnostic Criteria for Impulse Control Disorders

Pathological Gambling

Pathological gambling (PG) is characterized by a loss of control over gambling, deception about the extent of involvement with gambling, family and job disruption, theft, and chasing losses (DSM-IV-TR, 2000). Despite its high prevalence, PG often remains untreated. According to a report of the National Gambling Impact Study Commission (1999), 97% of problem gamblers in the United States fail to seek treatment. Although the history of gambling treatment extends over several decades, there is a surprising lack of reliable knowledge of what constitutes effective treatment for problem gambling. According to a critical review of the literature on the treatment of PG (Toneatto & Ladouceur, 2003), the interventions falling within the cognitive-behavioral spectrum have good empirical support at present.

PG is defined as persistent and recurrent maladaptive gambling that interferes with personal, family, or occupational functioning. The 10 criteria established by the American Psychiatric Association (DSM-IV-TR, 2000) can be used to obtain information regarding gambling-related behaviors, as well as the severity of gambling habits. These criteria also reflect the consequences of gambling and how it affects family, occupational/social/academic functioning, financial well-being, and legal status. Note that at least five of the ten criteria listed must be met for a diagnosis of PG.

DSM-IV-TR Criteria for Pathological Gambling

1. The gambler is preoccupied with gambling (e.g., preoccupied with reliving past gambling experiences, handicapping or planning the next venture, or thinking of ways to get money with which to gamble).

2. The gambler needs to gamble with increasing amounts of money in order to achieve the desired excitement.

3. The gambler has had repeated unsuccessful efforts to control, cut back, or stop gambling.

4. The gambler is restless or irritable when attempting to cut back or stop gambling.

5. The gambler gambles as a way of escaping from problems or of relieving a dysphoric mood (e.g., feelings of helplessness, guilt, anxiety, depression).

6. After losing money gambling, the gambler often returns another day to get even (i.e., "chasing" one's losses).

7. The gambler lies to family members, his therapist, or others to conceal the extent of involvement with gambling.

8. The gambler has committed illegal acts such as forgery, fraud, theft, or embezzlement to finance gambling.

9. The gambler has jeopardized or lost a significant relationship, job, or educational or career opportunity because of gambling.

10. The gambler relies on others to provide money to relieve a desperate financial situation caused by gambling.

Reprinted with permission from the Diagnostic and Statistical Manual of Mental Disorders, Text Revision, Fourth Edition, (American Psychiatric Association [DSM-IV-TR], 2000).

Kleptomania

Kleptomania (KM) is characterized by the repetitive, uncontrollable stealing of items not needed for personal use (DSM-IV-TR, 2000). Although kleptomania typically has its onset in early adulthood or late adolescence (McElroy et al., 1991), the disorder has been reported in children as young as 4 years old (Phelan, 2002) and in adults as old as 77 years old (McNeilly & Burke, 1998). Intense guilt and shame are commonly reported by those suffering from kleptomania. Items stolen are typically hoarded, given away, returned to the store, or thrown away. Many individuals with kleptomania (64% to 87%) have been apprehended at some time due to their stealing behavior (Grant & Kim, 2002a; McElroy et al., 1991). There is evidence from numerous case studies that a variety of CBT techniques are effective in the treatment of KM. CBT is favored over other approaches such as psychodynamic and psychoanalytic therapies, and the literature supports this (Grant, 2006). Studies to date suggest that CBT, when used in combination with medication, is more effective than medication alone. Large randomized controlled trials are lacking.

DSM-IV-TR Criteria for Kleptomania

1. Recurrent failure to resist impulses to steal objects that are not needed for personal use or for their monetary value.

2. Increasing sense of tension immediately before committing the theft.

3. Pleasure, gratification, or relief at the time of committing the theft.

4. The stealing is not committed to express anger or vengeance, and is not in response to a delusion or a hallucination.

5. The stealing is not better accounted for by conduct disorder, a manic episode, or antisocial personality disorder.

Pyromania

Although Pyromania (PY) is considered by some to be a rare disorder, a study of 107 patients with depression found that 3 (2.8%) met current DSM-IV criteria for pyromania (Lejoyeux et al., 2002), and a recent study of 204 psychiatric inpatients revealed that 3.4% (n=7) endorsed current and 5.9% (n=12) had lifetime symptoms meeting DSM-IV criteria for pyromania (Grant et al., 2005). Fire setting among individuals with pyromania often does not meet the legal definition of arson (Grant & Kim, 2007).

DSM-IV-TR Criteria for Pyromania

1. Deliberate and purposeful fire setting on more than one occasion.

2. Tension or affective arousal before the act.

3. Fascination with, interest in, curiosity about, or attraction to fire and its situational contexts.

4. Pleasure, gratification, or relief when setting fires or when witnessing or participating in their aftermath.

Compulsive Buying

Current research has found the prevalence of compulsive buying (CB) to be approximately 1.4% (Koran et al., 2006) in the general population, 1.9% of college students (Odlaug & Grant, 2010) and up to 9%

in individuals seeking psychiatric treatment (Grant et al., 2005). The problem typically begins in late adolescence, and a greater proportion of compulsive buyers are women. Compulsive buyers commonly have co-occurring depression and anxiety disorders, substance use disorders, and eating disorders. Co-occurring personality disorders range from 50%–60% (Black et al., 1998). Sufferers can experience a significant urge to engage in the problem behavior with little control over their actions (Frost et al., 1998). The act of buying may be experienced with feelings of excitement or euphoria, often followed by dysphoric mood, shame, and/or letdown once the buying experience is complete. The goal of the purchase may often have nothing to do with the actual item, but rather to alter one's mood. Compulsive buying behavior is often preceded by negative affect, including feelings of anger, boredom, and anxiety, with the purchase providing temporary relief (Miltenberger et al., 2003). Buying may occur year-round or happen in binges, with purchases for self or overindulgent purchases for loved ones. The purchases can occur in a range of venues, with Internet shopping adding significant flexibility and convenience for quick purchases. Common items purchased by compulsive buyers include clothing, shoes, jewelry, and electronics. Currently, there are no formal DSM criteria for CB. However, McElroy et al. (1994) have proposed the following:

Proposed Diagnostic Criteria for Compulsive Buying

A. Maladaptive preoccupation with buying or shopping, or maladaptive buying or shopping impulses or behavior, as indicated by at least one of the following:

1. Frequent preoccupation with buying or impulses to buy that is/are experienced as irresistible, intrusive, and/or senseless.

2. Frequent buying of more than can be afforded, frequent buying of items that are not needed, or shopping for longer periods of time than intended.

B. The buying preoccupations, impulses, or behaviors which cause marked distress, are time consuming, significantly interfere with social or occupational functioning, or result in financial problems (e.g., indebtedness or bankruptcy).

c. The excessive buying or shopping behavior does not occur exclusively during periods of hypomania or mania.

McElroy SL, Keck PE Jr, Pope HG Jr, Smith JM, Strakowski SM. Compulsive Buying: A Report of 20 Cases. Journal of Clinical Psychiatry. 55(6), 242–248, 1994. Copyright 1994, Physicians Postgraduate Press. Reprinted by permission.

Cognitive-Behavioral Therapy for Impulse Control Disorders (CBT-ICD)

Cognitive-behavioral therapy for ICDs aims to help individuals engaging in impulsive behaviors to understand all the facets of their problem in order to gain control over their behavior. The treatment helps them to stop or reduce the problem behaviors and to deal with the many consequences of the ICD. Individuals with an ICD should be better able to understand how their thinking drives their behavior, how to correct their impulsive thoughts, and how to develop healthy behaviors to replace the ICD behaviors. Through understanding the relationship between thoughts and behavior, individuals with an ICD will be directed toward discovering solutions that are appropriate for them. CBT exercises allow individuals with an ICD to acquire or develop new thought processes and behaviors that they can then apply in daily life. These exercises will also assist individuals in coping with events or emotions that trigger their desire to engage in their problem behaviors.

This guide is based on well-established CBT principles that have been applied to gambling (Ladouceur & Lachance, 2007; Petry, 2005), and will also be applied to other ICDs. Working with Dr. Ladouceur, we have modified many of his approaches to gambling to be applicable to an array of ICD behaviors. Research to date has focused primarily on the efficacy of CBT for PG. Following CBT treatment for PG (Sylvain, Ladouceur, & Boisvert, 1997), 80% of participants no longer present the characteristics of excessive gamblers. Its effectiveness has been proven by several randomized controlled trials (Grant et al., 2009; Sylvain et al., 2007; Petry et al., 2006; Ladouceur et al., 2001). Our CBT treatment program uses previously tested methods for PG and integrates those with cue exposure and motivational interviewing techniques (Grant et al., 2009). This has resulted in a CBT program that can be used for selected ICD problems using a total of six CBT sessions along with an optional family session. The CBT-ICD program addresses clinical issues characteristic of all the ICD problems, as well as the unique features of each (e.g., financial management unique to PG and CB, but not PY or KM).

Cue Exposure (CE)

A unique element of this treatment is the use of cue exposure therapy (CET) based on classical conditioning. CET, which is well validated in the treatment of fear-based problems (Foa & Kozak, 1986), has the goal of extinguishing the feared or learned response. The learned response (fear, panic) is extinguished through repeated exposure to a conditioned stimulus (dogs) in the absence of the feared consequence (not all dogs bite, I am safe). There is preliminary evidence, on the use of CET with addictions, that urges or cravings can be elicited using in vivo and imaginal exposure techniques (Carter & Tiffany, 1999). Cue reactivity to relevant stimuli (drug/alcohol) appears to be an important factor in addiction that can contribute to relapse (Cooney et al., 1997). CET studies conducted with PG (Symes & Nicki, 1997; Sodano & Wulfert, 2010; Echeburua, Baez, & Fernandex-Montalvo, 1996; McConaghy et al., 1991; Kushner et al., 2007) have reported positive findings, yet with few randomized controlled trials. The CET treatment approach used in this manual is based on findings from our recent work (Grant et al., 2009) and the work of Kushner et al. (2007), combining CET with negative mood induction (NMI). Kushner and colleagues (2007) used in vivo exposure in an actual casino with gamblers observing only, while listening to a pre-recorded imaginal exposure unique to each participant's negative consequences of gambling (NMI). Approximately two-thirds of the sample reported gambling urges while observing, and a subsequent decrease in urge with NMI. Grant et al. (2009) found that 77% of participants receiving imaginal exposure (IE) plus NMI, as part of a 6-session cognitive-behavioral therapy (CBT) program for PG, were able to maintain abstinence for one month, as opposed to only 27% of those randomly assigned to Gambler's Anonymous referral. For the CBT with IE + NMI group, among those participants who responded to therapy within 5 weeks, 94% maintained their response for 6 months.

Our findings reflect the use of CET as one of the key elements in our CBT-ICD program. The NMI involves focusing on the negative consequences of the problem behavior while the urge to engage in the problem behavior is active. The combination of CET plus NMI is believed to elicit an urge to engage in the problem behavior using problem-specific cues (e.g., sounds of the casino), as well as the relevant emotions experienced before, during, and after an ICD episode (e.g., euphoria before and during the ICD episode, and dysphoria or agitation post ICD episode). The method of CET + NMI will vary depending on the ICD. For example, ethical concerns would prohibit exposure to actual cues for certain problems (e.g., PG entering casino, unlimited access to credit cards for CB). The CET + NMI will be facilitated primarily via imagination, which allows for significant flexibility in activating urges and in identifying negative consequences related to the ICD.

Structure of Sessions

The treatment program described in this guide is directive. Each session of the treatment has a clear structure that takes the therapist and client through specific skills and then reinforces those skills through homework exercises. Homework is essential to mastering these techniques. This treatment is similar to taking piano lessons: if the person does not practice between lessons, they simply cannot learn to play the piano. Homework is akin to "practicing" between lessons. Each session will review the previous homework, new techniques for that session, and then new homework assignments for the following week.

Review of Past Week

The course of therapy is simple. At the beginning of each session, the therapist collects the client's completed self-observation form from the previous session and asks about the client's problem behaviors. No one will continue to do homework if it is ignored, and that is why the review of the homework is crucial. Self-monitoring of problem behaviors is a critical intervention to increase self-awareness. Self-monitoring helps the client and therapist identify the frequency of the problem behaviors, triggering events, urge intensity, level of control, and the negative consequences. Self-monitoring will be described as such to clients, to stress the potential benefits in managing their problem. Clients with poor insight into the effects of their ICD will likely benefit the most from this initial therapy assignment. Individuals with an ICD can be quite adept at cognitive and behavioral avoidance in order to manage negative affect and other consequences of their problem behavior. Self-monitoring, as well as other interventions in this program, is designed to increase awareness and ultimately help clients with an ICD to exert some control over the problem. Self-monitoring of the problem behavior is also a means for clients to monitor progress and change in this program, and helps in learning from mistakes when "slips" occur.

Homework Review

At each session, the therapist will complete an initial check-in with the client to review self-monitoring and therapy assignments from the previous session. The therapist will ensure that clients understand concepts within each session prior to presenting new material. Understanding these concepts is important, as each weekly assignment builds upon the next and is continuously reinforced throughout the treatment period. Clients will have approximately one week between sessions to practice new skill sets designed to manage their ICD. The therapist will establish expectations for therapy early on, and stress the importance of homework completion. Failure to complete therapy assignments will serve as an opportunity to evaluate barriers to full participation in the CBT-ICD program.

Homework Assignments

At the end of each therapy session, clients are given assignments to complete during the next week. The homework corresponds in theme and format with the chapters in the client's workbook. Therapists must be aware that certain crises may occur during therapy and that some flexibility in treatment may be needed. For example, someone with shopping or gambling debt may suddenly find out that their house is in foreclosure, or someone with kleptomania may be arrested. These crises may need to be addressed in lieu of the next session of homework. Many of the skills used to address a crisis can be well integrated into the cognitive piece of this treatment, as clients often need to learn how to cope with difficult emotional events without relapsing back into the ICD behavior. Because we have found that individuals with an ICD do not stay in treatment very long, each session needs to address as much information as possible. For clients with some cognitive limitations, or for those who feel easily overwhelmed, the sessions can be repeated or extended over a couple of weeks. In general, however, 6 sessions with the possibility of an additional family session are enough to impart the necessary skills for the client to gain control over their ICD behavior.

Use of Workbook

The CBT-ICD workbook is assigned to clients for use from assessment through the final session of the CBT-ICD program. Each session chapter includes objectives, psychoeducational information, and forms and worksheets individualized to specific session content. Clients are assigned to have the CBT-ICD workbook accessible throughout the day for the purposes of self-monitoring and completing therapy exercises. The therapist will emphasize the importance of using the workbook on a daily basis as assigned. The therapist can share the analogy of "cramming for a test" and the resulting consequences. Clients may have been able to manage with such short-term strategies in the past, and even succeed in doing so. However, long-term change in the ICD problem will only be achieved with daily, repetitive practice of therapeutic strategies using the CBT-ICD workbook. Upon completion of the program, clients will be encouraged to use the workbook as needed for relapse prevention.

Chapter 2   *Assessment*

(Corresponds to Chapter 1 of the workbook)

Introduction

The initial assessment includes ICD-specific measures as well as broad-based measures to identify comorbid conditions that can potentially interfere with the efficacy of the CBT-ICD program (e.g., bipolar disorder, alcohol or drug use disorders). Before beginning any intervention that aims to modify a behavior, the therapist must undertake a complete evaluation of the extent of the ICD problem, the repercussions of the problem behavior on the client's life (e.g., financial, social, psychological, legal, or familial), the presence of other mental disorders and addictions, the risk of suicide, etc. The use of questionnaires and of a diagnostic interview will allow the therapist to have a fairly complete view of the client's life situation.

The initial evaluation will also allow the therapist to determine the best way to approach the associated problems. We generally recognize four strategies for treating comorbidity:

1. Integrated treatment, where the same therapist treats all of the identified problems simultaneously

2. Parallel treatment, where two therapists treat different problems simultaneously

3. Sequential treatment, where the problems are treated one after the other

4. Individual treatment, where only one of the problems will be treated (Najavits, 2003)

For example, an individual suffering from bipolar disorder who reports excessive gambling only during manic episodes may no longer present with gambling problems once his mood is stabilized. Likewise, an individual with an alcohol addiction who steals only when intoxicated may no longer be considered to have an ICD once the alcohol problem is resolved. A good initial evaluation will allow the therapist to create a treatment plan that is adapted to the circumstances of each individual client.

Following the initial interview, the therapist will specify client goal(s) and motivation to stop the problem behavior. This step is important in order to know if the individual is ready to be involved and fully invested in the treatment of the ICD.

Early on in treatment, the therapist and client will work together to identify ICD triggers that increase the likelihood of clients engaging in impulsive behaviors. In order to begin helping clients with ICDs regain a certain degree of control over their lives, the risky situations unique to each client will be identified early on in treatment, and behavioral interventions will be suggested.

Pretreatment Assessment Objectives

The goals of the initial assessment are to:

- Assess the severity of the ICD problem, what brings the person to treatment at this particular time, and the person's motivation to change his or her behavior.

- Assess the repercussions of the ICD behavior and the person's perception of risk in engaging in the problem behavior.

- Assess related co-occurring medical issues, mental health problems, and other addictive behaviors.

The majority of clients who participate in the CBT-ICD program seek treatment when their behavior has started to substantially interfere with their lives. An assessment will be completed for each ICD to determine the severity (frequency and intensity) of the problem, as well as the consequences of engaging in the problem behavior. A detailed description of the assessment process for each ICD will follow. This initial assessment allows the therapist to individually tailor a treatment plan that meets the needs of each client.

The initial assessment consists of: diagnostics and symptom severity checklists, assessing the consequences of the ICD, medical and psychiatric comorbidity, motivation to change the ICD, and level of control over the ICD.

Diagnostic Interviews for ICDs

Before beginning the treatment, it is important to evaluate the nature and intensity of the problem. DSM-IV-TR remains the base of reference for diagnosing an ICD. It also provides a good idea of the dynamics of the ICD. Compulsive buying (CB) is an exception, because there are no DSM-IV-TR criteria currently established. However, the Structured Clinical Interview for DSM-IV-TR includes sections for proposed disorders, including CB. The diagnosis of pathological gambling (PG), as well as other ICDs, can be made with a structured clinical interview using the DSM-IV-TR criteria and being aware of the exclusion criteria (not better accounted for by another Axis I disorder). The following structured clinical interviews for ICDs, which are administered by the clinician, have been included in the Appendix of Assessment Measures:

- The structured clinical interviews for PG (SCI-PG; Grant et al., 2004), PY and KM (Grant, Kim, & McCabe, 2006).

- Minnesota Impulsive Disorders Interview (Grant, 2008).
  This allows for a screening of all ICD behaviors (including compulsive buying).

Severity of Illness Measures

The following measures provide a baseline assessment regarding the severity of the ICD in question. Some are self-reported, and can be mailed to clients for completion ahead of the initial assessment. Others are administered by the clinician. These scales take only a few minutes to use, and can give valuable information about the severity of the problem during the week prior to starting treatment. They also provide a baseline against which improvement can be measured during the course of treatment.

- Yale-Brown Obsessive-Compulsive Scale Modified for Pathological Gambling (PG-YBOCS; Pallanti et al., 2005) – clinician-administered

- Gambling Symptom Assessment Scale (G-SAS; Kim et al., 2009) – self-report scale

- Yale-Brown Obsessive-Compulsive Scale Modified for Kleptomania (KM-YBOCS; Grant, Kim, & Odlaug, 2009) – clinician-administered

- Kleptomania Symptom Assessment Scale (K-SAS; Grant & Kim, 2002b) – self-report scale

- Yale-Brown Obsessive-Compulsive Scale—Shopping Version (YBOCS-SV; Monahan et al., 1996) – clinician-administered

- Compulsive Buying Symptom Assessment Scale (CB-SAS) – self-report scale

- Pyromania Symptom Assessment Scale (P-SAS) – self-report scale

Assessment of the Consequences of ICD

The Consequences of the Impulse Control Problem is a 9-item measure used to identify (see Appendix) the negative consequences of each ICD. A thorough understanding of negative consequences of ICD will assist the therapist and client in developing a treatment plan. For example, individuals with PG report high rates of bankruptcy, divorce, unemployment and legal problems (Grant & Kim, 2001). Individuals with CB incur significant debt. Individuals with KM and PY likely have histories of arrests for stealing and/or fire-setting (Grant & Kim, 2002a; Grant & Kim, 2007). It is essential to understand these related problems, as they may affect the motivation to adhere to treatment and have an impact on the possibility of relapse.

Assessment of Comorbid Disorders

Comorbidity studies have found a strong association between ICDs and substance use disorders (including nicotine dependence), affective disorders, and anxiety disorders (Crockford & el-Guebaly, 1998; Grant & Potenza, 2006; Grant & Kim, 2007; Grant, Brewer, & Potenza, 2006; Black et al., 1998). Consuming alcohol or drugs can greatly reduce the willpower to resist impulsive behaviors. Some data has found that continued use of nicotine may negatively impact long-term abstinence for some ICDs. Each client's drug and alcohol problems will be assessed before initiating treatment. In cases in which clients are addicted to substances, appropriate referrals should be made. As is the case with almost any disorder, clients are unlikely to benefit from therapy until a drug or alcohol addiction is treated. In cases in which the impulsive behaviors occur only in the context of being under the influence of drugs or alcohol, clients may benefit from chemical dependency treatment alone. Regardless of level of use, you will need to review each client's drug and alcohol use to assess possible interference with treatment.

Affective disorders, such as depression and bipolar disorder, are frequently seen in patients with ICDs. Studies also suggest that individuals with ICDs have elevated rates of suicidal ideation and suicide attempts. Untreated bipolar disorder or depression may worsen ICD behaviors (e.g., someone steals more when manic; someone buys more frequently when trying to elevate a depressed mood) and needs to be treated prior to addressing the ICD behavior. Suicidal ideation is always a priority, and needs to be assessed and addressed at the initial evaluation, as well as throughout the course of treatment with the client.

Assessment of Motivation to Change

There is striking ambivalence on the part of people with ICDs. The clinician may not at first understand this dilemma. How can someone not want to stop such destructive behavior? Clinicians need to remember that although the ICD behavior has negative consequences, during the activity itself there can be an incredible "rush" or pleasure associated with it. For example, kleptomaniacs get a rush from stealing the object, although they may feel guilty immediately afterward; gamblers get a high from the sights and sounds of a casino, even if they regret their gambling a few hours later. It is the rush or high from the behavior that keeps the person engaging in the ICD behavior, over and over again. Consequently, individuals with an ICD may not want to seek treatment, may seek treatment only when forced by family or friends, or may want treatment today and not tomorrow. The motivation to stop the behavior may be present after a negative consequence, but once that consequence has resolved, the person may rethink his or her desire to stop the behavior. Because clients with an ICD may seek treatment immediately after experiencing a significant negative consequence from engaging in the problem behavior, but then drop out of treatment as soon as the urge is active again, it is best to assess their motivation to change, as it may interfere with adherence to treatment. Motivation for change may be assessed using the *University of Rhode Island Motivation for Change Assessment Scale* (DiClemente & Hughes, 1990). Please visit the following website for more information: http://www.uri.edu/research/cprc/Measures/urica.

Assessment of Control over Impulsive Behaviors

The client must describe the situations he considers the riskiest for him, and must then estimate the extent to which he believes he is able to resist the urge to engage in the problem behavior if he finds himself in one of these situations. This exercise will allow the therapist to determine which situations need to be an area of focus, and to create a behavioral intervention plan adapted to the client's needs.

ICD triggers will be unique to each client's ICD. For example, clients that gamble excessively may have a gambling urge triggered when they have access to money, have no accountability, and no alternate activity planned. Clients that shop compulsively may have similar triggers. Clients that engage in illegal acts, such as fire-setting or stealing, may be triggered by a mood state and/or the opportunity to engage in the illegal acts. The therapist will ascertain each client's unique triggers, and assess the client's confidence in being able to resist the urge to engage in problem behaviors.

Chapter 3 | *Session 1: Education and Motivational Enhancement*

(Corresponds to Chapter 2 of the workbook)

Materials Needed

- Completed initial assessment

- Motivation to Quit Impulsive Behavior form

- Daily ICD Behavior Diary

- Financial Spending form (if applicable to primary ICD)

- Financial Budget form (if applicable)

Session Outline

- Provide education about impulse control disorders

- Evaluate the client's motivation and provide motivational interviewing (Review client's ICD assessment)

- Provide overview of the treatment program

- Discuss the importance of self-monitoring and introduce the Daily ICD Behavior Diary

- Begin financial planning (if applicable to primary ICD)

After the initial assessment, begin Session 1 by educating the client about impulse control disorders. Many clients respond well to knowing that each ICD is an illness that has clear biological underpinnings, and that they do not indicate the presence of a character flaw. It is important to emphasize that although their ICD is an illness, clients *do* have control over how they respond to their illness.

An example that is often helpful for clients is the parallel to diabetes management. Clients are told that diabetes is an illness. No one chooses to develop diabetes, and people with both good and bad characters may develop the disease. However, having diabetes necessitates that the client take charge of his eating habits, that he change his lifestyle to accommodate diabetes, and that he does not put himself in situations where he may have problems with his blood sugar levels.

Educating the client means also discussing what is known about treating the primary ICD, the rates of remission if left untreated, and rates of relapse when treated. Clients are also educated about the role of significant others in their treatment and recovery, including the need to make healthy choices regarding what types of social activities they may need to avoid, and to identify people in their lives that represent healthy choices. Establishing or re-establishing these relationships with family or friends may be difficult for the client, given the emotional toll ICDs often take on the clients' significant others. This will need to be addressed, and will be discussed later in the manual.

For clinicians who want a greater background on ICDs, including their clinical aspects and outcomes from treatment, there are several books that may be useful (further suggestions are provided at the conclusion of this manual):

- Grant, J. E. (2008). *Impulse Control Disorders: A clinician's guide to understanding and treating behavioral addictions.* New York: W. W. Norton & Company.

- Grant J. E., & Potenza, M. N. (eds.). (in press). *Oxford Library of Psychology: Oxford Handbook of Impulse Control Disorders.* Oxford, UK: Oxford University Press.

- Aboujaoude, E., & Koran, LM. (eds.). (2010). *Impulse Control Disorders*. Cambridge, UK: Cambridge University Press.

- Ladouceur, R., & Lachance, S. (2007). *Overcoming pathological gambling: therapist guide.* Oxford, UK: Oxford University Press.

- Petry, N. M. (2004). *Pathological gambling: etiology, comorbidity, and treatment.* Washington, D.C.: American Psychological Association.

Patients or family members who want more information on ICDs might consider the following:

- Grant, J. E., & Kim, S. W. (2003). *Stop me because I can't stop myself: taking control of impulsive behavior.* New York: McGraw-Hill.

Motivation

It sometimes happens that clients seek treatment motivated by suffering some negative consequence from engaging in their impulsive behavior (e.g., caught stealing, gamblers losing a large sum of money, spouse finding out about compulsive shopping, etc.). Such motivation is generally not very conducive to therapeutic success. It is best to take some time to evaluate such a client's motivation to stop the impulsive behavior. As it is extremely difficult for most individuals with an ICD to stop their impulsive behavior, it is usually not sufficient that the client attends therapy sessions and talks about his problem. In order for the problem to be resolved, clients need to make enormous and active efforts between sessions. It is very important to establish each client's objectives and expectations with regard to treatment. For example, does the impulsive gambler, shopper, stealer, or fire-starter seek complete abstinence or moderation (e.g., what is often referred to as "controlled" gambling)? These initial expectations will determine what direction the treatment will take.

Motivational Interviewing

One way to enhance motivation for cessation of impulsive behavior is through motivational interviewing (MI), a series of counseling strategies developed by Miller and colleagues to enhance readiness to change (see Miller & Rollnick, 2002, for more information). MI is an interpersonal process that emphasizes the relationship between the therapist and the client. MI is based on the premise that the client has the primary responsibility for change. The therapist's role is, therefore, to present objective information to the client and allow him to decide for himself if he is willing and able to engage in treatment.

Feedback

Begin MI by providing the client with feedback on the structured clinical assessment. MI should include a review of the client's readiness for change, and an assessment of his primary source of motivation (internal vs. external). For individuals with ICDs, feedback about financial status, debt, relationship problems due to the ICD, and how family and other relationships have been affected, are used to demonstrate the impact of the ICD on the client and others.

Responsibility

MI emphasizes the client's responsibility for change. This should be stated explicitly, so that clients can decide what they can do with the objective feedback and other information provided by the therapist. Following is an example of how a therapist can provide objective feedback to a client suffering from compulsive buying:

> *Based on your financial problems and marital troubles due to compulsive buying, the best thing you could do is get your shopping under control. However, I know this is difficult and that issues around your spending are complicated. What you decide to do about your spending is up to you.*

In addition, you should offer support and encouragement to each client as she thinks about quitting, and when she decides to quit.

Advice

It is important for you to clearly state your recommendations regarding the impulsive behavior cessation and the need for abstinence (or, in the case of shopping, a more controlled approach). Be sure to provide information regarding the fact that most clients with an ICD find it difficult to engage in the impulsive behavior in a controlled manner. Rather, a more realistic and healthy outlook would entail complete abstinence from the behavior. Of course, in the case of compulsive buying, a goal of abstinence is not really practical, as all people may need to buy things from time to time. In that case, controlled spending is the goal. You may wish to provide a recommendation like the following:

> *In my opinion, it would really help all aspects of your life if you were to quit your impulsive behavior. But what you decide is up to you.*

> [If client is a compulsive buyer] *In my opinion, it would really help all aspects of your life if you were to have greater control over your spending. What you decide, however, is up to you.*

This allows the client to retain control, but still provides a message of support.

Many clients with an ICD have tried unsuccessfully to quit their impulsive behavior in the past. Providing a list of strategies for quitting or reducing behavior can help clients select the strategies that are most appropriate for their present circumstances, and the ones they are most likely to follow.

Empathy

An empathic style is one in which the therapist shares an understanding of each client's experiences and meaning, through reflective listening. Using empathy allows the therapist to express his or her genuine desire to understand each client's situation, thoughts, values, and beliefs. Clients with ICDs have likely encountered significant negative feedback and judgment from family, significant others, and friends as a result of their problem behaviors. In our clinical experience, participation in therapy may be the first time individuals with ICD receive empathy and support for their problem behaviors, which can have significant implications for addressing defensiveness and facilitating a willingness to change.

Self-Efficacy

Self-efficacy is the client's self-confidence in his ability to successfully carry out a specific task. The goal of MI is to enhance self-efficacy. This can be done by focusing on each client's ability to handle specific circumstances without engaging in the impulsive behavior (for example, dealing with a stressful day at work and not shoplifting). By developing strategies for dealing with difficult circumstances, a client's confidence in his or her ability to function without the impulsive behavior will increase.

Motivation to Quit Impulsive Behavior Form

You will work together with the client to complete the *Motivation to Quit Impulsive Behavior* form in Chapter 2 of the client workbook. Refer to the sections that follow for descriptions of aspects of impulse control problems that you can use to guide discussion. Inquire about the consequences of the impulsive behaviors with open-ended, non-judgmental questioning (e.g., "tell me about how your gambling, buying, stealing, or fire-setting has affected you").

Positive Aspects of Impulsive Behavior

Each problem behavior will include unique positive effects. Shoplifters describe the feeling of power from stealing, the sense of getting something for nothing, and the feeling that they are in control of their lives. Gamblers often mention the escape from frustrations or problems, and having a good time. There are similarities across ICDs, such as the experience of an urge to engage in the problem behavior and the excitement or rush associated with the behavior.

Negative Aspects of Quitting the Impulsive Behavior

You will discuss with the client what he will miss about the impulsive behavior. The negative aspects of each client's impulsive behaviors will also be unique to each ICD, and share some common aspects. Compulsive buyers need to let go of the special feeling they get from buying merchandise. The gambler needs to accept that he has lost money, along with the opportunity to buy other things with that money or pay bills. The shoplifter may feel powerless without the act of stealing. Fire-setters may miss the adrenaline rush and excitement they get from starting fires. Recognizing these aspects of the behavior are important, as the clients may relapse if they cannot replace these lost, unhealthy aspects of their behavior with new, healthier options. It is important to stress that everyone wants to feel a rush, feel important or powerful, or feel engaged. The feelings are not the problem. The expression of those feelings, however, can be healthy or unhealthy. What the client is attempting to do in this treatment is to find healthy outlets for these feelings.

Negative Consequences of Impulsive Behaviors

The list of negative consequences is long for all of the ICDs—loss of self-esteem, shame, depression, isolation, loss of trust by others, interpersonal conflicts, financial difficulties, legal problems, wasted time, harm to others, and occupational problems. Clients with an ICD are usually aware of these negative consequences, although they often do not want to admit them. Many clients may initially say that they are unsure if their behavior is really a problem. When asked in detail about multiple areas of their life (relationships, work, etc.) and how the ICD behavior may be affecting these areas, most clients are able to provide multiple examples of the negative aspects of their behavior. Therefore, the goal for both the therapist and the client is increased awareness, on a daily basis, of all the consequences of the ICD behavior.

Advantages of Stopping Impulsive Behaviors

Why should someone want to stop a behavior that is thrilling or exciting? The advantages of stopping an ICD behavior are not always easily seen by the client. A sense of control over one's behavior may theoretically sound good, but what does this actually mean to the client? One way to represent the advantages is to have the client think about both short-term and long-term advantages. If the positive aspect of quitting will only be realized a year later (for example, the client will have financial stability in a year), that may not be enough to counterbalance the immediate rush the behavior provides. Therefore, thinking of short-term (i.e., today, this week, this month) benefits (i.e., no fights at home, no reprimands from the boss) as well as long-term (i.e., 1-year, 5-year) benefits (i.e., financial stability, retirement) can be more useful.

We suggest that clients complete the *Motivation to Quit Impulsive Behavior* form in Chapter 2 of the workbook, and then review the consequences on a daily basis. Clients need to be reminded on a more regular basis of all the consequences of their impulsive behaviors.

Overview of Cognitive-Behavioral Therapy

The therapist will provide the client with a basic introduction to cognitive-behavioral therapy (CBT) and how it is used to treat ICDs. You may wish to use the following sample dialogue to provide the introduction. A detailed description of the program is also included in the client workbook.

> *CBT is based on the scientific fact that our thoughts cause our feelings and behaviors, and by changing the way we think about a situation, we can modify our emotional response and our behaviors. CBT is structured with the goal of therapy being able to help clients unlearn their unwanted reactions, and learn a new way of reacting. Questioning the thoughts that are unique to each person's problem (e.g., what do you expect to happen when you engage in this behavior?) is a critical component of CBT. Our thoughts are simply hypotheses, or theories that can be questioned, tested, and corrected if*

inaccurate (e.g., "I always expect that buying something will make me feel special"). When people understand how and why they are doing what they do, they can change the behavior. Thinking about one's behavior or changing behavior, however, is not enough. You will be expected to complete assigned readings, self-monitoring exercises, and to practice skills between sessions. The goal of this CBT-ICD program is to help you achieve control over your impulsive behaviors. Changing your thoughts and behaviors should lead to control.

By agreeing to participate in treatment, you are agreeing to attend 6 weekly sessions, with follow-up visits offered as needed. In Session 1, we will evaluate your motivation to quit the impulsive behavior, and get you started on monitoring your urges and behavior. In Session 2, we will create a plan for managing your specific behaviors. If you have a problem with gambling or compulsive buying, we will create a financial plan. If you suffer from kleptomania, we will create a plan for dealing with stolen merchandise. In Session 3, we will work to identify your triggers and implement healthy behaviors to reduce the risk of impulsive behaviors. In Session 4, we will begin exposure therapy, and in Session 5, we will work on changing your erroneous thoughts about your behavior. Relapse prevention will be addressed in Session 6. There is also an optional Session 7, where you can invite family members to join so they can learn about your disorder and discuss how they can help you manage it.

Self-Monitoring

As briefly discussed in Chapter 1, daily self-monitoring is critical to treatment success. Refer the client to the Daily ICD Behavior Diary in Chapter 2 of the workbook, and explain that completing the diary will be an ongoing assignment throughout the duration of the program. Encourage the client to photocopy the form from the workbook, as he will need multiple copies. Additional copies can also be found in the workbook Appendix.

The client will use the diary to record aspects of his impulsive behaviors every day. The *Daily ICD Behavior Diary* is general enough to be used by all clients, but also includes items specific to certain ICDs. Individuals with an ICD tend to underestimate the extent of their behaviors, and the diary allows for increased self-awareness of behavior. In addition, as the person progresses through therapy, the diary provides an easily quantifiable means of assessing improvement. Every day, clients will describe their sense of control over their behavior and document the frequency of their behavior.

Financial Planning

Clients that are dealing primarily with PG and CB will be assigned to begin self-monitoring their weekly and monthly spending. Once the spending pattern has been established, the therapist will assist clients in developing a budget that fits their finances. A financial budget will serve to increase awareness of gambling and shopping debt, and facilitate planning for debt repayment. A regular review of finances will potentially discourage future impulsive behaviors. Financial monitoring forms are provided for the client in Chapter 3 of the workbook.

Homework

✎ Encourage the client to review the Motivation to Quit Impulsive Behavior form on a daily basis as a way to maintain motivation to change.

✎ Instruct the client to begin daily self-monitoring using the Daily ICD Behavior Diary in Chapter 2 of the workbook.

✎ The client who suffers from PG or CB should be instructed to complete the Financial Spending form in Chapter 3 of the workbook, and bring it to the next session for review.

Chapter 4

Session 2: Financial Planning, ICD Trigger Planning, Plan for Managing Stolen Goods

(Corresponds to Chapter 3 of the workbook)

Materials Needed

■ Daily ICD Behavior Diary

■ Financial Spending Form

■ Financial Budget Form

■ Strategies I Will Use to Manage My Finances form

Session Outline

■ Review past week and homework

■ Review spending (for PG and CB clients)

■ Review strategies for managing finances (for PG and CB clients)

■ Review strategies for management of stolen goods (for KM clients)

■ Review strategies for managing fire-starting urges (for PY clients)

Past Week and Homework Review

Review the client's completed Daily ICD Behavior Diaries from the preceding week. Use the diaries with the client to describe and better understand:

■ The intensity of the desire to engage in the ICD behavior and the sense of control over the behavior

- The extent of the behavior

- Associated feelings or thoughts

Financial Planning

Problem gamblers and compulsive buyers will present with a variety of financial challenges ranging anywhere from credit card debt, to home foreclosure, to bankruptcy. In this session with your PG and CB clients, you will discuss current financial management strategies to assess how they have been managing their money, and what needs to be done in the future to have greater control over finances. In order to increase self-awareness of spending and money management in general, clients will begin to keep a weekly and monthly budget of all expenses. This may be difficult for the client, as many people do not like to know how much money they spend or on what. Therefore, there may be some resistance to this plan. The client needs to understand that finances may be a trigger for future relapse, and addressing the financial problems will be more beneficial than ignoring it. Also, the client should be reminded that *not* addressing financial issues does not make them go away or improve. A challenge for many clients is a lack of accountability for their spending. Finances can be reviewed with spouses, significant others, family, or whomever will serve as a support for the client. The use of online banking is another option for clients to easily produce reports and monitor spending. A budget will be particularly helpful as a guide for clients in paying off gambling or shopping related debt. You may wish to provide the client with a spreadsheet for recording daily financial transactions. You must review the client's budgets on a weekly basis in order to facilitate the development of new financial management habits. Clients with more severe financial problems may require the support of a financial counselor and, in some cases, an attorney for bankruptcy filing.

Monitor Spending

The first step in developing a budget that fits each client's individual needs is to begin monitoring spending for a minimum of two weeks. As per the homework assigned last session, PG and CB clients should have spent the last week recording their spending using the Financial Spending Form in Chapter 3 of the workbook. Review the client's spending activity over the past week, and then ask the client to monitor spending for at least 2 additional weeks in order to come up with approximate numbers for developing a budget.

Budget

Provide the client with guidance in developing an individualized budget, once expenses and regular spending have been reviewed. Initially, the client will be accountable to the therapist for having developed a budget. Ideally, the client should designate a support person who will have a copy of her budget and will regularly check in with the client on budget adherence. You will, however, check progress in following the budget in each session, regardless of the client's support system.

In planning a budget, there are several factors to consider. Is the client making maximum payments on debts? If not, why not? Clients with outstanding ICD-related debt will be encouraged to use more of their discretionary money (after expenses are paid) to pay down debt. The client will also need to consider cutting back spending in certain areas in an effort to pay down debt. For example, instead of going out to eat, the client may have to eat at home and plan a menu each week. Clients may have to reconsider family trips and vacations. Smaller cuts may be made in order to free up money, such as canceling Internet access or cable television. It is important to keep in mind that ICD clients struggle with "cutting back" or controlling their behavior. It will take some time to adjust to dealing with money more conservatively. The most important outcome of developing a budget will be clients' increased awareness of incoming/outgoing money.

Available money is the main element that contributes to the persistence of spending or gambling. The more money in the client's possession, the more likely the client is to engage in gambling or spending behaviors. Consequently, clients need to limit access to money.

How can clients better manage their access to money? The client can temporarily have a loved one or close friend manage her money. This needs to be done with clear and strict rules between the parties, so as to avoid future arguments and relationship problems. Also, a loved one or friend needs to understand what this arrangement may entail and be aware of it before agreeing to it. To manage someone's money may be too large an emotional burden for many people. Alternatively, the client may consider using a financial consultant, often set up through her banking service. A financial consultant may be quite useful for the client facing bankruptcy.

Clients often feel humiliated when they give up control of their finances to someone else. They feel that they are being treated as a child, or being punished for their behavior. Working through this sense of shame is important, so that it does not lead to relapse. Also, clients need to be reminded that the new financial relationship is only short term, and that the client will regain control over finances once the ICD behavior is under control.

If clients settle their financial situations, they will be less preoccupied by the idea of money and will be in a better position to undergo therapy. Compulsive buyers may be less inclined to spend frivolously when they are more aware of their financial situation and feel in control. Gamblers may better realize that gambling further is not the way to fix their present financial problems. If clients are unwilling to use one of these strategies, you can suggest some simple means that are applicable to certain situations in order to reduce the client's urge to gamble or overspend. For example, clients should carry only a limited amount of pocket money; cancel credit cards; get rid of bank debit cards; instruct friends and family that they are not to lend them any money; arrange for any checks received to be automatically deposited into their bank account (usually savings accounts are safer); and, arrange alternative plans on paydays (such as going to a movie with friends or having dinner with family).

Work with the client to choose financial management strategies that are right for her, and have her list them on the form provided in Chapter 3 of the workbook.

Managing Stolen Goods – For the KM Client

Clients that struggle with KM may not have significant financial problems, but rather may have a surplus of merchandise worth differing amounts. Compulsive shoplifters frequently keep, hoard, discard, or return stolen items, with the latter indicating that individuals may actually profit financially from the thefts committed. You will work together with your KM client to prevent him or her from benefiting financially from stolen merchandise. The focus of this session for the KM client is development of a plan to deal with stolen merchandise. Encourage the client to identify possible alternatives for getting rid of the stolen merchandise.

Plan for Dealing with Stolen Merchandise

Following are some options for dealing with stolen merchandise:

- Identify charities of interest, to include charities that accept donated merchandise. Clothing is accepted by most organizations (e.g., The Salvation Army, Goodwill, Dress for Success, Lupus Foundation, etc.).

- Have the client inform his or her family of the plan to discard stolen items. Clients will need some measure of accountability outside of the therapist–client relationship.

- Identify local schools that may use certain items (e.g., electronics, office supplies). Clients may run into obstacles when donating to certain programs. There may be requests for warranty or proof of purchase.

Have the client use the space provided in Chapter 3 of the workbook to identify the charities to be donated to, and when the donation will be made. Remind the client to ask a friend or family member to accompany him or her when making the donation. Tell the client that he or she will be required to present a receipt for the donated items at the next therapy session.

Managing Fire-Setting Urges – For the PY Client

Clients that are deliberately setting fires will begin identifying behavioral interventions prior to Session 3. Clients struggling with this impulsive behavior will need to identify their ICD triggers sooner rather than later. You may begin this process with the client by having him identify and discard all potential fire-setting items in his home, including matches, all forms of lighters or torches, flammable substances, etc. However, because fire-starting implements are readily accessible, this approach is far from foolproof. As noted with other ICDs, a loved one or significant other will need to be actively engaged in preventing this problem habit. Specific behavioral interventions will be explored in Session 3. For now, you will work with the PY client to identify his support system and who will serve as his primary support during this treatment program. You may consider use of a role-play exercise with the PY client to practice asking loved ones for help. For example, "I know how much my fire setting has harmed our relationship, but I am trying to quit. Your involvement in my treatment will be essential for me to make healthy changes."

Homework

✎ Instruct the client to continue completing the Daily ICD Behavior Diary in Chapter 2 of the workbook. The client may make photocopies as necessary, or use the additional copies provided in the workbook Appendix.

For the PG or CB client:

✎ Have the client continue monitoring weekly spending using the Financial Spending Form in Chapter 3 of the workbook.

✎ Encourage the client to begin filling out the Financial Budget Form in Chapter 3 of the workbook.

✎ Have the client review the completed Strategies I Will Use to Manage My Finances form, and implement strategies reviewed in session.

✎ For the KM client – have the client implement the plan for dealing with stolen merchandise.

✎ For the PY client – have the client identify members of his support system and begin identifying triggers for fire-setting.

Chapter 5 | *Session 3: Behavioral Interventions*

(Corresponds to Chapter 4 of the workbook)

Materials Needed

- Daily ICD Behavior Diary
- Controlling Impulsive Behaviors Questionnaire
- Controlling ICD Triggers form
- Life Categories form

Session Outline

- Review past week and homework
- Help the client begin to identify ICD triggers
- Introduce problem-solving skills for managing triggers
- Review leisure skills and set goals for leisure activities

Past Week and Homework Review

Review the client's completed Daily ICD Behavior Diaries from the preceding week. Use the diaries with the client to describe and better understand:

- the circumstances that resulted in the impulsive behavior
- the triggers (emotions, events, etc.) that caused the client to gamble/spend money, set fires, or steal

If your client has problems with gambling or compulsive buying, be sure to review his weekly spending and budget. Did the client identify a support person to assist in financial management? Did the client begin to implement strategies to manage his finances? If homework was not completed, spend some time troubleshooting why the client had problems completing the assignments.

ICD Triggers

Clients will begin to identify external triggers that provoke the urge to engage in impulsive behaviors. It would be unethical and unfair to ask clients to put themselves in situations where they have clearly demonstrated a lack of control. Gamblers oftentimes request being banned from casinos. Compulsive buyers can abstain from any shopping without a loved one to hold them accountable. Individuals with kleptomania may need to avoid stores, particularly when they are on their own. In cases where clients have been caught stealing in specific stores, they are likely to be banned already, and would be watched by security. Clients that are starting fires may need to eliminate all exposure to fires—for example, not monitoring news or police scanners for occurrence of fires, and not viewing material (e.g., movies, media, chat rooms) related to fires. Clients have little ability to manage their impulsive behaviors during the early stages of treatment, and must stay away from unnecessary "tests" of their ability to abstain.

Self-exclusion is, without a doubt, the first strategy to employ in order to avoid exposure to ICD triggers. For gamblers, many casinos have a process by which the person can self-exclude. For other ICD behaviors, self-exclusion (for example, for compulsive buyers or kleptomaniacs from certain stores) will be accomplished through their own efforts. Clients will likely again face ICD triggers in the future, but it is not recommended during the acute stage of quitting, before they have some skills to cope with urges and/or possible "thinking errors." You must work together with the client to identify unnecessary and avoidable ICD triggers.

Strategies for Managing ICD Triggers

Pathological Gamblers (PG)

Gamblers frequently report that they gamble at the same time of day on specific days of the week. Because most people generally take the same route home, certain triggers (e.g., billboards) may trigger the desire to gamble, and the gambler may feel unable to prevent himself from gambling. Suggestions for the gambler may include the following:

- Change driving routes to avoid driving past gambling establishments or billboards advertising them on the way home.

- Establish a carpool with coworkers, family, or friends. Doing this will reduce the temptation and ability to gamble.

- Cancel membership in any casino "rewards" programs and make sure that the client is removed from casino mailing (including email) lists. Gamblers often report being triggered by "free" rooms or slot machine credits from casino mailings.

- Avoid going to places where one can gamble. If the client goes to bars, he should avoid bars where there are pull-tabs or other gambling opportunities.

- As with compulsive buyers, pathological gamblers will be asked to consider leaving all credit and debit cards with a trusted friend or family member, or in a secure place (e.g., lockbox or safe) when leaving home each day.

- Plan alternate activities for payday. If receiving a paycheck is a common trigger, compulsive buyers and pathological gamblers need to plan activities in advance with a loved one or friend.

Compulsive Buyers (CB)

Compulsive buyers may shop online late at night when family members are asleep, or early in the morning once everyone has left for the day.

It is suggested that a spouse or loved one adjust security settings on the computer to prevent this behavior. Other strategies include:

■ Avoiding "window shopping."

■ Using shopping lists to focus on shopping only for essentials.

■ Because most compulsive shoppers prefer to shop alone, suggest only shopping if the person is accompanied by a family member or friend.

In addition to leaving credit and debit cards at home or with a friend, it is advisable that the shopper carry only a small amount of cash and the amount should be limited to the essentials on the shopping list. This will reduce the chance for impulsive purchases.

If the person primarily shops online, suggest that he remove computers from the home, and/or delete credit card information from the computer and set security blocks for shopping websites. In the event that it is unrealistic to remove the computers from the home, the passwords on the computer will be important, and/or the compulsive buyer may need to be restricted to computer use only in the presence of his support person.

Impulsive Shoplifters (KM)

If the person suffers from kleptomania, you should suggest that she stay away from the stores from which she typically steals, and perhaps stay away from all stores in general.

If the person tends to steal at the same time of the day (e.g., Friday night after work), suggest other activities she can engage in instead (e.g., going to a movie or having dinner with family or friends).

Because going to stores with someone may reduce the chance of stealing, suggest that the client only go to stores only if someone accompanies her.

The urge to steal can also be triggered by aversive emotions or distress, in which case stealing can serve as a tension release or, at the very least, a temporary distraction. Help the client to identify problem-solving strategies to effectively cope with uncomfortable emotional distress, such as communicating with a loved one about what is upsetting at the time.

It can also be helpful to review the consequences of stealing (e.g., getting caught, going to jail, etc.) before entering a situation that may trigger the urge to steal. Clients will need daily practice reviewing the consequences of stealing in order to have an increased awareness of this competing information when it is most important (i.e., urge is high, and in a high-risk situation).

Compulsive Fire Starters (PY)

Along with clients with other ICDs, compulsive fire starters may engage in their impulsive behavior whenever they have down time. Develop a plan for the client to engage in alternative leisure activities during free time. These activities should be exciting or thrilling, to replace whatever feeling the client reported from fire-setting. Replacing fire-setting with something dull or boring will not help.

Have the client avoid being left alone when the conditions are ideal for triggering desire to set fires. At the very least, the client should have access by phone/text/email to loved ones or friends, when feeling most at risk to set fires. There needs to be some communication with the support person to help the fire-setter become more objective about the consequences of acting on the impulse to set fires.

Restrict access to anything related to fire-setting—lighters, matches, gasoline, etc. Have the client enlist the help of a trusted friend or family member to rid his or her immediate surroundings of items that may facilitate engagement in fire-setting activities.

In the initial stages of managing the fire-setting problem, access to fire-related stimuli via television, movies, computer should be restricted if, in fact, such stimuli reliably trigger the fire-setting urge. You must also assess whether the fire-setter has access to police scanners, or in some way is tracking the location of fires.

Fire-setters may also need to alter driving routes or stay away from remote and/or public areas with an excess of abandoned buildings or lots.

Therapist Note:

■ *It is unrealistic to plan for clients with ICD to never be exposed to their ICD triggers in the future. The clients that we treat are adults and will eventually transition into having control of money again and will enter situations that previously served as triggers for impulse control problems. You will review relapse prevention strategies with the client in the final session. However, the controls that are set in place during treatment to ensure limited exposure to the ICD trigger must remain until clients have demonstrated new insight and increased control over their ICD. The therapist and client will discuss a plan for gradually giving back privileges to the client to engage in situations independently. This topic will be explored in more detail in the final session.* ■

Significant Others / Friends who May Serve as ICD Triggers

You will need to work with clients who typically engage in impulsive behaviors with others (e.g., clients who have a gambling or shopping "buddy") to develop a plan for resisting invitations to engage in impulsive behaviors. This step is especially important for those clients who gamble or shop with friends or family. One option is to use role-play activities to help you strengthen the client's assertiveness skills. Have the client practice refusing offers to engage in problem behaviors.

Another strategy for combating pressure from others to engage in impulsive behaviors is to help the client learn how to disclose his ICD behavior to friends and family. Someone close to the client who knows about the ICD can be a valuable ally when the client is trying to resist other people's pressure to engage in certain behaviors. Regardless of the dynamics in certain relationships, clients must direct others not to invite them to engage in the impulsive behaviors they are trying to quit.

When assertive communication fails to inhibit certain friends and/or significant others' unhealthy behavior, the client may need to consider a temporary or permanent break from such relationships. You can also provide support and guidance to the client in role-playing this challenging assertion with friends and significant others.

Relationship Difficulties

People with ICDs often isolate themselves because of their impulsive behaviors. Friends and family may also make efforts to distance themselves from the person with the ICD, due to diminished trust, inability of the person to follow through, constant problems with money, and/or legal problems. Impulsive behaviors can place great strains on relationships. For example, gamblers and compulsive shoppers that make frequent requests for money to cover debts, and neglect to pay back friends and loved ones, may find themselves alienated from the very people they need for support.

We offer an optional family session (see Chapter 9) to begin to work with clients in regaining the trust of their loved ones. In cases in which clients have repeatedly failed in attempts to quit and/or manage their ICD, they will have to prove to loved ones that recent efforts will be successful. Family members and friends may not be aware of the client's impulsive behavior, because many people keep their disorder secret. Clients that live otherwise "normal" lives and then act outside of their normal persona by setting fires, stealing, shopping compulsively, or gambling compulsively will likely find it difficult to disclose their behavior to loved ones. Not all friends and loved ones will understand and be supportive of the client's ICD, and relationships may change as a result. However, we do not advise clients to inform their employers of their behavior problems unless absolutely necessary.

Other Behaviors, Mood States, or Problems That Contribute to ICD Behaviors

ICDs are essentially *behavioral addictions*. This description is useful, as it suggests that people with these behaviors may also have other addictive behaviors, such as drinking or overeating. In the case of alcohol, drinking often contributes to poor decision making, with an inability to assess long-term consequences. In the case of ICD behaviors, drinking alcohol may make the decision to engage in the ICD behavior more likely, and the ability to consider the consequences less likely. If drinking is a problem in its own right, it needs to be addressed either before or simultaneously with the ICD.

Mood may also contribute to ICDs. When a person is stressed or depressed, he is less likely to attempt to inhibit the ICD behavior. "To heck with it all" becomes a common thought when work, family, or financial stress is extreme, or when feeling depressed. If this type of thought is endorsed by the client, you should consider using cognitive-behavioral strategies for mood or anxiety problems, in addition to the sessions for the ICD behavior.

If other problems are contributing to the ICD behaviors, problem solving may be useful in reducing the ICD behavior. Having the client write questions and answers to better clarify the problem (e.g., What exactly is bothering me? If I'm concerned about finances, what exactly about my finances bothers me?) are often useful in slowing down the thoughts and behaviors, allowing more time to problem-solve. Writing also allows the client to list possible solutions to the problems.

Developing Healthy Behaviors

For many people, the ICD behavior they are engaging in takes the place of activities that they used to enjoy doing. Once the client stops engaging in the impulsive behavior, however, he may find that he has significant free time on his hands and little to do. Because boredom may trigger a relapse, dealing with this newfound free time is important. Developing healthy behaviors to replace the ICD is crucial.

Have the client brainstorm activities and interests he pursued before the ICD consumed most of his time. What were the client's passions and hobbies? For example, did the client enjoy playing sports, volunteering, or exercising? Was the client involved in his church or other place of worship? Clients need to remember activities that they have neglected or completely abandoned as the ICD behavior became increasingly important in their lives.

Have the client use the *Life Categories* form in Chapter 4 of the workbook to list activities (new or otherwise) that he would like to engage in, now that he is getting the ICD under control. This form is used as a part of a well-validated treatment approach for people suffering from depression, called *behavioral activation* (Dimidjian, Martell, Addis, & Herman-Dunn, 2008). Rank ordering the activities allows clients to begin with moderately challenging activities in each of the life categories, and work their way up to the most challenging activities to take on. As noted earlier, it is easiest for clients to start with activities they already have some familiarity with and possibly increase activities they are already engaging in. Be sure the client is specific in creating a timeline for attaining the goal (e.g., goal attained in 1 month), as well as specifying how much time will be spent on the activity (e.g., 1 hour per day, Mon–Fri). Clients should list activities they can do on their own, as well as those that require the presence of other people.

The types of pastimes clients seek out are of little importance. The important thing at this point is to help the client fill free time in order to discover new interests, while reducing the risk of relapse. In the case of gamblers and compulsive shoppers, do not forget that a part of the money that was lost or spent will be used to cover expenses for healthier objectives with positive repercussions.

Support Groups

In addition to engaging in leisure activities, clients may use support groups to combat ICD triggers.

Participation in self-help groups like Gamblers Anonymous (GA), Debtors Anonymous and Shoplifters Anonymous may be helpful. Clients will find some support and encouragement among people who have experienced the same difficulties. Some clients will not feel comfortable sharing their problems in a group situation, or may have concerns that group discussion may focus only on "reliving" current or past episodes of impulsive behaviors. In such cases, clients may have concerns about urges being triggered by such discussion. Clients are nevertheless encouraged to attend several different meetings in order to find one that "fits."

In conclusion, there are many spheres in which to behaviorally intervene, and the proposed strategies are numerous. Behavioral strategies, used in conjunction with the correction of erroneous thoughts with regard to impulsive behaviors, increase the effectiveness of the intervention and allow clients to attain and maintain abstinence. These two approaches effectively complement one another and address the ICD from the maximum number of possible angles.

Homework

✎ Instruct the client to continue completing the Daily ICD Behavior Diary in Chapter 2 of the workbook.

✎ Encourage the client to begin implementing healthy behaviors to combat the ICD triggers identified on the Controlling ICD Triggers form in Chapter 4 of the workbook.

✎ Have the client complete the Life Categories form in Chapter 4 of the workbook, and begin engaging in leisure activities.

For the PG or CB client:

✎ Have the client continue monitoring weekly spending using the Financial Spending form in Chapter 3 of the workbook.

Chapter 6   *Session 4: Imaginal Exposure*

(Corresponds to Chapter 5 of the workbook)

Materials Needed

- Daily ICD Behavior Diary

- Audiotape and recorder to record imaginal exposure

- Imaginal Exposure Script form

- Imaginal Exposure Rating Form

Session Outline

- Review past week and homework

- Develop and record imaginal exposure

Past Week and Homework Review

Review the client's completed Daily ICD Behavior Diaries from the preceding week. Check to make sure the client began managing ICD triggers by implementing healthy behaviors, engaging in leisure activities, and utilizing the problem-solving method.

Imaginal Exposure

In this session, you will spend approximately 20 minutes having the client describe a typical scene, in detail, in which she engaged in her impulsive behavior, including all the senses as well as thoughts, feelings, behaviors she experienced. You will record the content on the Imaginal Exposure Script form provided on page 64, and subsequently audiotape it during the session. The script can also be assigned as homework prior to the exposure session, in order to save time. A copy of the Imaginal Exposure Script form is provided for the patient in Chapter 5 of the workbook.

External stimuli may include the sounds (e.g., slot machine, fire crackling, noise of fellow shoppers), smells (e.g., fire and cigarette smoke, scent in stores), and activity (e.g., fellow gamblers, watching for security cameras, music in background, sounds of others approaching) in the situation described. Each client will describe the unique features of his or her impulsive behavior. For example, gamblers will typically describe their type of gambling and details about their game of choice. A slot player may describe the graphics and sounds of his favorite machine, and gambling strategies that may involve superstitious thinking (e.g., picking a machine that has been played because it is due to "pay off"). Compulsive buyers may describe their shopping venues of choice, as well as the times of day they like to shop and the goal of the shopping outing, if any. Compulsive shoplifters may describe the type of store or establishment they typically steal from, and fire starters will likely describe the type of fire-setting situation they most commonly engage in.

Ask the client to describe the ICD trigger that led to the impulsive behaviors. Examples include: getting paid (for gamblers and shoppers); having too much free time; conflict with a friend, family member, or work colleague, etc. Be sure to capture the client's self-report of mood, thoughts, behaviors, and feelings before, during, and after a typical impulsive behavior episode. The consequences of the different ICD can occur to clients at different time points. All clients with an ICD will experience some increase in excitement either before or during the episode, and the negative consequences may be realized immediately afterward or may be delayed. The goal of imaginal exposure for ICDs is to introduce stimuli that are incompatible with the pleasurable aspects of the impulsive behavior (e.g., "I feel relief and excitement in the short term, but my problems don't go away and I feel increased distress for days after an episode")—a process called *negative mood induction* (NMI). The urge must first be activated during an exposure, which will consequently activate erroneous beliefs or cognitions. The competing information or negative consequences are most effective when the client is already focused on the pleasurable aspects of the impulsive behavior. As homework, clients are asked to listen to a recording of the imaginal exposure repeatedly, until their urge to engage in impulsive behaviors is decreased by approximately 50% of the peak urge reported during the exercise (e.g., peak urge of 90 reduced to 45 post-exposure). The client is asked to rate the pre-exposure urge, listen to the tape, and then to record the peak urge rating (noted during the exposure, and finally the post-exposure urge). Have the client use the Imaginal Exposure Rating Form in Chapter 5 of the workbook to record urge ratings.

Encourage the client to use healthy coping strategies during the exposure. Coping behaviors will be introduced in the exposure recording, after the triggers and negative consequences are introduced. After reading the script of the client's impulsive behavior experience and introducing the negative consequences of the client's impulsive behavior, you will describe a healthy coping behavior that the client can use to combat urges. For example, you may instruct a PG client to imagine that she has just been paid, which is typically a trigger for gambling, but instead of going straight to the casino after work, the client calls a supportive friend and makes plans to go to dinner instead.

Conducting Imaginal Exposures

During imaginal exposure, ask the client to be seated, close his or her eyes, and listen to the following instructions:

> *Today you will be imagining you are acting out your impulsive behavior via imagination. I'll ask you to close your eyes so that you won't be distracted. Please try to picture this scene as fully and as vividly as possible, not like you're being told a story, but as if you were experiencing it right now, at this moment. Every few minutes I will ask you to rate your urges on a scale from 0 to 100. Please answer quickly and don't leave the image. The purpose of the exposure is to initially increase your urge to act impulsively by describing a typical episode of impulsive behavior for you. Once the urge is active, we*

*believe the impulsive behavior related beliefs will also be active
(e.g., This will be fun; I will win this time and walk away; This new
TV is exactly what I need to cheer me up; I am too good at this to get
caught). This will be followed by the introduction of information
incompatible with the desire to engage in the impulsive behavior
(e.g., negative consequences). The information that is incompatible
with the pleasurable aspects of your impulsive behavior will possibly
decrease your urge to engage in the behavior. The exposure will
conclude by focusing on healthy coping strategies you may apply when
experiencing an impulse control related urge.*

Record the client's urge every 5 minutes on the Imaginal Exposure
Rating Form provided on page 65. The client will do this for herself
when she practices exposure for homework. If you find that the client's
urge ratings decrease over the course of the exposure, you may wish to
provide feedback such as, *"You see, as I told you, urges decrease if you just
continue to avoid acting on them."…"I want you to note that your impulse
control related urges are much less than at the beginning of the session."…
"As you can see, the more we confront this situation and avoid acting on
urges, the weaker the urges become."*

If urges to engage in the impulsive behavior do *not* decrease much during
the course of the exposure, you may wish to say something like, *"Today
your urges persisted. This happens occasionally. I want you to continue at
home exposing yourself to the taped situation, just the way we do it in session,
at least twice daily."… "Today your urges did not decrease by much. We will
continue to work on this issue until it gets easier."*

Imaginal exposures are greatly effective for helping clients prepare to
deal with their ICD triggers in real life. Following are some sample
imaginal exposure scripts tailored to specific ICDs.

Sample Imaginal Exposure Script for PG

*It's Friday and I have been looking forward to gambling all week.
<Ask client to rate his urge.> I am thinking about gambling right
now. My urge is <ask client for rating>. Work has been quite stressful
and it will feel good to escape for awhile and have some fun at the*

casino. I am bringing $200 and I have to leave the casino when that is gone. The money should last me maybe 2–3 hours. I hope the money can last a little while longer so I don't have to leave so soon. Driving to the casino, I notice my heart flutter slightly and I have butterflies in my stomach. I can hardly wait to get there. I am thinking about sitting down at my favorite machine, and hope that it is available when I get there. I thought of an excuse before today to tell my spouse where I will be—an after-work gathering. As I approach the casino, I notice the lights outside, my excitement increases and I drive a little faster. After parking my car, I get out and walk into the main entrance of the casino and feel a rush as I hear the ringing of slot machines and the hustle and bustle of people. I immediately head over to my bank of slot machines. I'm excited to see that one of my favorite machines is open and I take it as a sign that I am going to win tonight <insert name and description of client's favorite machine>.

My urge to gamble is at <ask client for rating> *and there is no way I would turn back at this point. I plug $10 into the machine and before I know it I have $50 in the machine. I win a few spins in a row and begin to increase my bets. I am still excited and hopeful that I can walk away with some winnings. The machine is not paying off, so I look for machines other gamblers have been playing that may be due to pay. I have been at the next machine for 30 minutes and I am out the $200 I brought. I head over to the nearest ATM and withdraw $200 more. I continue to lose on whatever machine I choose, and make two more trips back to the cash machine for $100 and $200, respectively. I continue to chase my losses, feeling disgusted with myself for staying so long and not having any control. My stomach feels sick and I have a headache. My urge to gamble is decreasing* <ask client to rate urge> *and the excitement has gone and I am now more focused on my anxiety.*

Move on to a description of the negative consequences of engaging in the impulsive behavior.

I planned to get home by 9pm and it is now midnight. As the gambling outing ends, I am walking away from the casino in disbelief. I planned to stay for a short time and gamble a small amount. Only now do I realize how much I took out of my bank

*account, and I have to think of an excuse to give my wife. I smell
like smoke, realize I have not used the bathroom for several hours,
and I have a raging headache. I am quite irritable, tired, and upset
with myself for letting this happen again. When I get home, my spouse
is upset with me and we argue before going to bed. I can't fall asleep
and I continue to replay the gambling in my head. I can't believe that
I didn't walk away. I am aware that I will be unable to pay my bills
because of my gambling. The next day I am not able to enjoy much.
I feel distant from my spouse and guilty for lying about gambling.
This has been a typical gambling episode based on the past year.
The benefit I get from gambling is short-lived, and I continue to
gamble increasing amounts of money, causing more financial
problems. The more I gamble the more conflict there is between
my spouse and me.*

Move on to a description of healthy coping.

*I can also imagine another scenario that did not result in me
gambling. I call my brother on Tuesday and let him know I need to
make plans for the weekend because I am concerned about gambling.
I will have dinner with my brother and his family and watch some
movies Friday night. On Saturday, I will commit to helping a friend
with a house project, and we plan to go out with mutual friends that
evening. I imagine myself still having the urge to gamble, but it is
tolerable and it passes. I am enjoying the company of my family and
friends. I remind myself that I always feel worse after gambling, and
if I stay involved in healthy activities, the good feeling will last longer
then a gambling outing and I am not doing any harm. I have to
continue to remind myself of the negative consequences of gambling,
and of the opportunities (socializing, self-improvement) I have when
I abstain from gambling.*

Generate similar scripts for other ICDs and include specific details.
Clients will often leave out relevant information that may help to
increase the urge to engage in the impulsive behaviors. Consequently, it
is vitally important for the therapist to properly identify ICD triggers
for each client and incorporate them into the exposure script. The
therapist will ask clients about all relevant triggers before and during an
episode of ICD behavior. Often, the thoughts about acting out the ICD

behavior and the planning will be just as urge-inducing as being engaged in the ICD behavior.

Sample Imaginal Exposure Script for CB

> *I have unlimited time to do what I want this afternoon. My spouse is at work, I am near some of my favorite stores, and I have credit cards with me. I can just window shop for awhile and maybe I will buy something if I find a good deal. I enter a store and notice the hustle and bustle of customers coming and going with shopping bags. Everyone seems happy and in a good mood, enjoying the music that is playing in the background. The smells in the mall <ask client to describe smells (e.g., perfume, food court, etc.)> hit me, and always put me in a good mood. I feel excited about finding something new, and can't wait to browse the clothing selection, and will definitely check out the shoe department. I notice a mild rush of adrenaline and I am not thinking about other responsibilities or consequences of purchases I will likely make. I had coffee right before shopping and feel lots of energy to shop. I am expecting that a purchase will further enhance my mood and help me feel good about myself.*

Move onto a description of the negative consequences of engaging in the impulsive behavior:

> *I am also aware of how quickly the urge and the excitement of a purchase decreases immediately after shopping, followed by feelings of shame and regret. I will not likely even wear the article of clothing I purchased, and the clothing will likely end up in my overcrowded closet with everything else I have ever bought and not worn. I am creating more debt with this purchase, and I am tired of dealing with the debt collectors and my poor credit rating. Once my spouse finds out I made this purchase, and he will, there will be yet another argument and he will continue to not trust me.*

Move on to a description of healthy coping.

> *Today I will be in the area where I typically shop uncontrollably, and must have a plan of how to abstain before I leave the house. I will buy*

groceries in an area away from the shopping mall. I will review our
current debt and expenses with my spouse. When I leave home, I will
have on hand the amount of money I will need for groceries, and will
have a grocery list. As a treat after running my errand, I will plan to
go for a walk with a friend and catch up. I remind myself of how
I will feel as our family gets closer to paying off my shopping debt and
using the money for vacations or accumulating savings for the kids'
college or our retirement. If I need to purchase something, I will think
about it and discuss it ahead of time with my spouse or significant
other, until I can objectively determine wants vs. necessities. I am
feeling better about the time regained not having to think about my
shopping or shopping related debt. I am more aware of how
overwhelmed I was most of the time being preoccupied with fighting
the urge to go shop, or covering up my purchases once I did shop.
I don't have to lie anymore, all family members are aware of my
problem and they are supportive in helping me manage this problem.
I am spending more time with family free of my shopping related guilt.

Imaginal Exposure Scripts for KM and PY

Work with KM and PY clients to identify all the triggers that contribute
to their impulsive behaviors. They can imagine their exposures to end
with getting caught, or they can simply imagine the possibility of being
caught and how that would affect them. The exposure can include
clients successfully stealing an item or setting a fire. This will likely
be necessary in order to activate an urge to engage in the behavior.
After having the client imagine the scene, introduce the negative
consequences.

For KM Client

Begin by having the client describe the steps that lead up to stealing and
what she is noticing as the episode begins.

I am thinking about running some errands. I don't have any plans,
have some downtime, and my spouse is at work and my children are

at school. I will be in the vicinity of my favorite store where I usually steal. It is a large discount clothing store and I know the security system is not that great because I have stolen many times at this store and not been caught. I am thinking about what the kids may need. I tend to steal things that the family needs, and sometimes take items that might look good on me. I can afford to buy most of the items that I steal, but feel like most clothing items I like are overpriced. I leave for the store and notice the excitement as I approach the store.

I feel intense excitement and a thrill of evading getting caught. I enter the store and quickly I am in the middle of several clothing racks. The store is moderately crowded and no store clerks in sight. I know where the cameras are, and they are easy to avoid. I see a nice blouse and immediately think it is way too expensive, but it would look really nice on me. I take a quick glance and easily slip the item in my oversized purse. I pretend to be shopping while I am using one hand to hide the item. I look up, no one seems to have noticed me. I go to the children's clothing area and see a pair of pants that would look good on my daughter and she needs a new pair of pants. These pants are also overpriced, and I search for a lower-priced item and switch the tag for the jeans, so I pay much less. Switching the tags really isn't stealing, right?! I feel justified in changing the price tag because I believe the item is overpriced. At least the store will be getting some of my money; then I will not feel so bad about taking the blouse. I approach the store clerk to check out and pay for the pair of jeans I switched prices on. I feel the adrenaline rush again. There is no other rush like it. I am only thinking about the act of stealing and what I need to do to complete it. I am not thinking about how this behavior could have negative consequences. I don't imagine I will be caught. I've never been caught and reported to the police before, and I've done this many, many times. I have been caught by stores in the past, but only asked to pay a fine and I was banned from one store. The store clerk comments that I found a good deal, we make small talk about our children. I feel some guilt because the store clerk seems really nice and decent. I leave the store slowly, aware that I could still get caught. I know stores have to catch me in the act, and if they did not catch me in the store, they could confront me as soon as I leave. I look around for security to see if anyone is following me. Nobody in sight, I get out the door and to my car, and feel a huge sense of release and then some of the guilt.

Move onto a description of the negative consequences of engaging in the impulsive behavior:

Once I get to my car, I feel the sense of relief of not being caught, and having got away with something. My thinking quickly shifts to the tremendous risk I just took. It is no longer just me suffering negative consequences; it is my entire family, most importantly my children that will suffer the embarrassment of their mom getting caught stealing. How can I look my daughters in the eye and tell them what is right or wrong when I can't control my own behavior? What kind of role model can I ever be for them if I can't act like an adult? What is wrong with me? Do I need attention, why do I need such a thrill? I am risking everything. The next time I get caught, the police could get involved, my spouse would find out I am still stealing and, eventually, my girls would find out. They would lose all respect for me. When I steal, I think I am very smart about it and nothing is wrong with getting a good deal or taking something that is overpriced. Now, after leaving the store, I feel completely out of control, and I feel shame. Once I feel this guilt, I notice that I spend less time with the girls, I am more irritable, less talkative and not myself. I make an excuse and go to bed early. The blouse I stole goes in the closet and the excitement of having stolen it is completely gone.

Move on to a description of healthy coping.

I have some downtime, my spouse is at work and the kids are at school, and I am feeling the need to treat myself for all my hard work. Usually that would mean I go and steal something. I was aware that I would have downtime today, so I planned ahead and scheduled time with a friend. We are going biking. I recently took up mountain biking. I have always been a biker, but never tried off-road biking on trails. The trail that I have been riding with a friend has a lot of downhill sections, which can be quite challenging. It is not the same rush that I feel when I steal something, but it can be quite exciting. I had to invest in a new bike, but the benefits greatly outweigh the cost. After biking, I have lunch with my friend, and I get home in

time to prepare to meet the kids when they get home from school.
I don't have to deal with the guilt of stealing, and I am more engaged
with the kids and my spouse. I feel good taking care of myself and have
a much more positive outlook. I feel in control for once. If I have to
enter a store, I now recognize that I always need to have a plan for
what I need to purchase. I also try to bring a loved one with me,
especially at times when I am feeling a stronger urge to steal. I still
enjoy looking for a bargain, but now I pay for it like everyone else,
and I am becoming more accepting of this change.

For PY Client

Begin by having the client describe in detail the steps leading up to a
fire-setting episode.

I am bored, nothing planned, nothing on television looks interesting,
and I start to think about some of the fires that I have set. I replay
them in my head, getting away with it. I think about how I have
planned for setting a fire so I don't get caught. The planning is very
exciting, having a strategy, having an entry and exit plan. I can go
over this for hours, but eventually I have to act on my ideas. I set out,
have materials in my trunk, lighter, matches, gasoline, jars, old rags
and towels to use to set the fire. I have dark clothing on and wear
gloves. I drive by an abandoned building, out of the way, no chance
of anyone being there or being able to see me. I could set a fire, keep it
in control, and nobody will be the wiser. There is the possibility that
there is a security guard on duty, but I can watch out for that. It is
exciting to think about how high the flames will burn, the sound of
the fire, the heat from the fire, the smell of the lighter fluid, and the
image of the flames flickering in the wind. I find the perfect spot,
where I could set the old building on fire and get away easily. I park
my car and get the materials. I notice myself feeling more excited as
I get closer to starting the fire. I pour the gasoline onto the floor and
one of the walls. I use a match from a distance to light the gasoline.
I stay as long as I can to watch the fire start and climb the wall, the
excitement builds. I love to watch the flames and feel the heat from
the gas igniting. I quickly make my exit and leave in my car. I have

a police scanner in my car, and I park a safe distance away, waiting for the emergency call. Once I get home, I look for the story on the news and want to record any stories about MY FIRE. In a way, the attention makes me somehow feel important, like I am better than other people.

Move onto a description of the negative consequences of engaging in the impulsive behavior:

It does not set in until the next day what I did. I could have hurt myself, or strangers that might have been in the building. The fire fighters that have to manage the fire could be harmed. It is so addictive, seeing the fire, and it is exciting to set, but what if I get caught? I would lose my job, and I have a pretty comfortable living. My urges don't disappear after I set a fire. I need to set more and more fires, and don't feel like the satisfaction lasts, it is always short-lived, I keep taking more and more risks. I was caught when I was a minor and the fire was pretty insignificant, but did get me into trouble with my parents. If I get caught now, it will be hard to recover from. What if I hurt someone next time? I can't let this escalate any more. What if my friends and family find out? They would not understand, they will treat me differently, lose all respect. I don't ever think about what could go wrong when I am planning or setting fires. I just think about getting away with it and how exciting it will be. I am out of control!

Move on to a description of healthy coping.

I am home from work and planned for downtime. I usually get into trouble with fire-setting on the weekends. This weekend I have planned activities. I joined a fantasy football league, and now spend part of every Sunday with friends. The investment is minimal, not as serious as more advanced leagues, and it is a lot of fun. I have plans to take a rock-climbing class with a friend during the week. On Saturday I have made a commitment to my nephew to take him to swimming class. My brother and his wife have been bugging me for a long time to spend some time with him, and I finally agreed. Once his swimming class ends, we will spend another 2–3 hours together. I have gotten rid of all fire-setting materials in my home, and all fire-related videos/movies, etc. I sold my police scanner and have

*started making an annual donation to a local firefighters association.
I avoid driving in areas I used to set fires, and try to account for
downtime. I continue to explore leisure activities. I am more aware
of feeling in control, and feel less guilty as more time goes by without
my having set a fire. I am considering going back to school. I feel a
sense of freedom now that I am not constantly preoccupied with
thoughts or images related to fire-setting. I still have an urge on
occasion, but I plan for potential triggers. I feel more in control.*

Imagery Guidelines

Many clients may not have experience with imagining scenes as vividly
as is necessary to evoke their urges for impulsive behaviors. It is therefore
useful to try a few practice imaginal scenes to "warm up" for the planned
exposures. Use the following directions to help the client learn imaginal
exposure skills:

> *The aim of imaginal exposure is for you to imagine yourself in
> the situation we are describing and feel as if it were really happening
> to you. Not like it's a story being told, but like you're living through
> the situation and are aware of the thoughts, feelings, sights, sounds,
> and sensations. To do this, you have to be good at vivid imagination,
> and this takes practice. So, let's start with some easy scenes to get
> warmed up.*

Ask the client to close his or her eyes and focus on what you are saying.

> *Picture yourself on a beach in the middle of summer. It is very hot and
> you can feel the sun beating down on your skin—particularly on your
> shoulders and back (pause). There is a gentle wind blowing off the sea
> and you smell the salty air. Do you have the scene? How vivid is it?
> Describe how you feel.*

Encourage the client to maintain the scene.

> *Now, you hear the waves crashing against the sand, and you hear
> people playing and seagulls crying out. It is very bright. Do you have
> the image? Are you there? Just practice keeping the image (pause).*

Alternatively, you may use the following practice scene with clients.

Imagine yourself outside on a crisp November morning. There is a cold breeze that you feel on your face, and it is very quiet except for the rustling of leaves on the ground. The sun is very bright and you can barely look in the sky. Tell me what you see when you look around. Describe how you feel on the inside.

Therapist Note:

■ On rare occasions, clients actively conceal ICD activity which has been specifically prohibited by the therapist. In cases like this, confront the client with this discovery in a matter-of-fact way and without anger. Its implications for treatment outcome should be emphasized. You may wish to say something like the following:

I understand from your wife that you were gambling/shopping/stole something/set a fire this weekend. She called to tell me because she felt I needed to be aware of it. What happened?

It seems that right now you aren't able to stop your impulsive behavior. Every time you relieve your impulsive behavior urges, you prevent yourself from learning that the urges would have declined eventually. ■

Homework

✎ Instruct the client to continue completing the Daily ICD Behavior Diary in Chapter 2 of the workbook.

✎ Encourage the client to continue implementing healthy behaviors to combat the ICD triggers identified on the Controlling ICD Triggers form in Chapter 4 of the workbook. Healthy coping strategies include engaging in leisure activities and utilizing the problem-solving method introduced in session 3.

✎ Have the client practice imaginal exposure twice in the morning and twice in the evening, or four total daily exposures, and record urge ratings on the Imaginal Exposure Rating Form in Chapter 5 of the workbook. The client is assigned to continue the imaginal exposure exercise daily until there is a 50% or greater reduction in peak urge rating or until the next therapy session, whichever happens first.

For the PG or CB client:

✎ Have the client continue monitoring weekly spending using the Financial Spending Form in Chapter 3 of the workbook.

1. Describe a situation where you typically would engage in your impulsive behavior. Describe exactly what you imagine happening step-by-step and your urge to act impulsively. Describe as many details about the experience as possible, including all your senses, what you imagined/or did see, hear, smell etc. If relevant, would you be using alcoholic, drugs, smoking etc? What physical symptoms are you aware of (e.g., rapid heart rate, sweating) and what negative consequences do you anticipate from your impulsive behavior? Finally, imagine coping with the urge and resisting it.

    ----

2. Symptoms: Record all symptoms that accompany this feared situation.

Difficulty breathing		Nausea/abdominal distress		Muscle tension		Other	
Racing/pounding heart		Chest pain/ discomfort		Dry throat			
Choking sensation		Hot/cold flashes		Restless/pacing			
Numbness/tingling		Sweating					
Shakiness/trembling		Faint/dizziness					

Imaginal Exposure Rating Form

0	10	20	30	40	50	60	70	80	90	100
None		Mild			Moderate			Severe		Extreme

Date (Exercise)	Pre-tape Urge	Peak Level of Urge	Post-tape Urge
Morning Practice 1 (am)			
Morning Practice 2 (am)			
Evening Practice 1 (pm)			
Evening Practice 2 (pm)			

Chapter 7 | *Session 5: Impulsive Beliefs: Cognitive Therapy*

(Corresponds to Chapter 6 of the workbook)

Materials Needed

- ABC Log
- Disputing Impulsive Beliefs form

Session Outline

- Review past week and homework
- Help the client to identify thinking errors associated with the ICD
- Introduce the ABCs of impulsive behavior
- Help the client work through an ABC Log and Disputing Impulsive Beliefs form in session
- Define and discuss notions of "chance" (for PG client)

Past Week and Homework Review

Review the client's completed Daily ICD Behavior Diaries from the preceding week. Check to make sure the client continued to practice managing ICD triggers by implementing healthy behaviors, engaging in leisure activities, and utilizing the problem-solving method. Also check that the client listened to the imaginal exposure recording at least four times each day and recorded urges on the Imaginal Exposure Rating Form. Review the client's peak urge ratings from daily exposures to ensure there was an expected decline in the ICD urge following several repetitions. In the case of a client not practicing, or practicing on a limited basis, the urge ratings may have not changed markedly. Under such circumstances, instruct the client to repeat the exposure tape until there is at least a 50% or greater reduction in the peak urge rating. A decrease in the urge ratings following imaginal exposure provides some evidence of insight, and of the client's ability to tolerate internal triggers with less reactivity (i.e., "I can think about it, experience the urge, and don't have to act on it").

Identifying Thinking Errors

In this session you will work with the client to identify the thinking errors and erroneous beliefs related to his or her ICD behavior. In an effort to elicit possible thinking errors, you will guide clients in identifying their specific thought process before, during, and after an episode of impulsive behavior. It has been our experience that clients' thought processes change markedly in the life cycle of an episode of impulsive behavior (e.g., from optimism/hope/excitement pre-event, to a complete focus on the positive effects of the behavior during an event, to possible regret/shame/remorse post-event). You and the client have already begun this process in the imaginal exposure session. Clients have learned behavioral interventions to limit their exposure to cues that can trigger impulsive behaviors. The next step in the process is helping clients to understand that behind every action there is a thought, and that thoughts provoke our reactions (urge, emotion) and influence impulsive behavior.

All clients with an ICD will report differences in their thinking, and can likely find ways to "rationalize" their behavior during an episode of impulsive behavior. Clients may make efforts to quickly forget or ignore the negative consequences of the behavior. It is your job to help identify the client's tendency to distract himself from the negative consequences of his impulsive behavior. One way to accomplish this is to have the client identify and record impulsive behavior episodes using the ABC Log in Chapter 6 of the workbook (more details are provided in the next section). The very act of recording is expected to increase awareness and help clients to understand thinking errors. The goal of using cognitive therapy for an ICD is to correct thinking errors in the moment the thoughts are happening and influencing behavior—when the urge to engage in impulsive behavior is high.

ABC's of Impulsive Behavior

First, define the ABCs of impulsive behavior as follows.

A = Activating Event (ICD trigger)

B = Impulsive Beliefs

C = Consequence (urge and behavior)

D = Dispute Impulsive Beliefs

E = Effect Change

Activating Event

The activating event is what triggered the client's urge to engage in the impulsive behavior. Refer back to Chapter 5 (Session 3), where you first worked with the client to identify triggers. Have the client list the activating event in the appropriate column of the ABC Log in Chapter 6 of the workbook.

Belief

The **'B'** of impulsive behavior stands for *belief* and is how the client thinks his impulsive behavior will affect his mood. Will it excite him or make him happy? Will he win? Will she get away with stealing? Provide guidance by having clients rate the degree of certainty that an impulsive belief is valid on a scale of 0–100, with 0 signifying no certainty at all, and 100 signifying absolute certainty that the impulsive belief or prediction will happen.

For example:

- "I am 85% certain that I will gamble $200, stay for 2 hours, and walk away with winnings."

- "I am convinced (90%) I can purchase 1–2 items, spend what I plan to, and will use the items I purchase."

- "I am 100% certain that stealing a few items will be exciting and fun, and that I will not get caught or suffer any negative consequences."

- "I can set a fire, keep it under control, and not cause any harm (90% certain)."

Once the impulsive belief is identified and recorded in the appropriate space on the ABC Log, the belief can then be disputed with evidence.

Consequence

The '**C**' of impulsive behavior stands for *consequences*. Ask the client to rate the intensity of his urge to engage in the impulsive behavior (using a scale of 0–100), as well as what he did (i.e., did he engage in the impulsive behavior?), on the ABC Log.

Dispute

Using the Disputing Impulsive Beliefs form in Chapter 6 of the workbook, have the client identify evidence for and against his impulsive beliefs. Help the client to take an objective view. The exercise of evaluating impulsive beliefs will ultimately bring to light short-term vs. long-term effects of the ICD, with clients likely being focused on "short-term benefits" while ignoring the long-term consequences. The evidence will include identification of objective events that have occurred in the past, versus what clients "think or feel" will happen. It may be helpful to consider the following suggestions when helping clients to dispute impulsive beliefs.

- Review illusion of control. For example, how much time did the client spend engaged in the impulsive behavior relative to what the client set out to do? How much is spent, gambled, or stolen relative to what each client planned?

- Consider mood/affect changes. How long does relief from distress last when clients are using their impulsive behaviors to manage their moods? Review with the client mood changes before, during, and after an impulsive behavior. Clients often report time-limited positive affects from engaging in the impulsive behaviors, and the negative effects can persist until the next episode. This can result in a "vicious cycle" of clients constantly chasing that initial high from their impulsive behavior, while mood continues to worsen (e.g., depressive episode, anxiety disorder), along with all other aspects of their lives.

- Also, clients can consider past experiences of having urges and resisting the urge. The point being, the urge will pass and the clients do not need to act on the urge.

Once clients have identified evidence for and against erroneous impulsive beliefs on the Disputing Impulsive Beliefs form, the evidence will be transferred back to the ABC Log, along with the alternative beliefs. Clients will also rate certainty in the dispute that was developed using the 0–100 rating.

Effect Change

The Effect Change column of the ABC Log is an opportunity to evaluate the *effectiveness*, or 'E' of impulsive beliefs, of the disputing evidence, and alternative beliefs. Clients will then rerate their degree of certainty in the original impulsive belief, as well as their urge to engage in the related impulsive behavior (B and C columns of the ABC Log).

Figures 7.1–7.4 show completed ABC Logs for clients with different ICDs.

Please note that the examples provided in this guide do not take into consideration how long it takes for clients' urges to diminish. Clients can expect that it will take a lot of practice in order to effectively challenge their impulsive beliefs to the extent that it helps to prevent or discourage them from engaging in impulsive behaviors. The cognitive intervention is combined with behavioral strategies to make it less convenient for clients to engage in their problem habits. PG and CB

Date/Time	A Activating Event (ICD Trigger)	B Belief (Rate certainty 0–100)	C Consequence (Rate intensity 0–100)	D Dispute (Rate certainty 0–100)	E Effect Change (Rerate certainty in belief and intensity of urge 0–100 in Columns B and C)
Monday 8 am	I received coupons in the mail for my favorite store and then started to plan when I could get to the store, maybe right after work, I could even get out early to shop a little longer and find a good deal.	I will be able to stop when I plan to, spend the amount I want, and walk away with purchasing what I planned to. Rating = 80 Revised rating = 35	I will not spend uncontrollably. Rating = 80 Revised rating = 30	When I examine the evidence, I know that I quickly forget about all the limits I have set for myself, I have rarely if ever stopped shopping when I planned to, always spend more than I plan to, and buy way more than I intended. The next time I think about shopping I need to remind myself that I have limited control over my spending and it would be irresponsible to even go window shopping. I always feel guilty after excessive shopping, especially when my significant other sees the bill, causing more arguments about our increasing debt. Rating = 90	After considering the dispute, I would rerate how certain I was in the initial belief, as well as the intensity of my urge to shop.

Figure 7.1

Sample ABC Log for CB Client

Date/Time	A Activating Event (ICD Trigger)	B Belief (Rate certainty 0–100)	C Consequence (Rate intensity 0–100)	D Dispute (Rate certainty 0–100)	E Effect Change (Rerate certainty in belief and intensity of urge 0–100 in Columns B and C)
Saturday 9 pm	Bored, thinking about finding a store where I could grab something, nothing planned for tonight, everyone is busy, notice excitement when I think about the thrill of stealing something.	I know stealing will be exciting, will bring me relief from boredom, and I will get away with it. Rating = 80 Revised rating = 20	I will not get caught. Rating = 80 Revised rating = 30	I do experience excitement and a rush of adrenaline before and during a stealing episode. I have had several close calls where store attendants have come close to catching me in the act. That increases the excitement in the moment, but as soon as I get home, I just add this item to the stack of other stolen merchandise. Every time I look at the stuff I have stolen, I feel a mix of guilt and shame. Each time I steal, I seem to need to take more risks to get the same level of excitement, which could result in me getting caught, jeopardizing my livelihood and relationships. The excitement quickly fades each time and then I am back to feeling bored, maybe even depressed. Each theft brings less and less satisfaction and I am getting closer to being caught. When I am not stealing something, I am constantly thinking about it, and this is interfering with other important parts of my life. Stealing is holding me back from commitment to work and relationships. The risk/excitement is not worth the cost. Rating = 100	After considering the dispute, I would rerate how certain I was in the initial belief, as well as the intensity of my urge to steal.

Figure 7.2

Sample ABC Log for KM Client

Date/ Time	A Activating Event (ICD Trigger)	B Belief (Rate certainty 0–100)	C Consequence (Rate intensity 0–100)	D Dispute (Rate certainty 0–100)	E Effect Change (Rerate certainty in belief and intensity of urge 0–100 in Columns B and C)
Friday 5:30 pm	End of the week, nothing planned, stressful at work, have $300 available and I could drive by the casino on my way home from work. Spouse has an after-work gathering, so I will have time to go and get home before he is done.	I am sure I will win Rating = 80 Revised rating = 40	I will walk away with winnings Rating = 75 Revised rating = 30	Now that I consider all the evidence, I don't find it so believable that I will be able to win, and walk away with the winnings. I also recognize the laws of chance are working against me and usually favor the house. I will get home late and my spouse will be upset with me again, he has threatened to leave me if I don't quit gambling and giving all of our savings away to the casino. Rating = 85	After considering the dispute, I would rerate how certain I was in the initial belief, as well as the intensity of my urge to gamble.

Figure 7.3

Sample ABC Log for PG Client

Date/Time	A Activating Event (ICD Trigger)	B Belief (Rate certainty 0–100)	C Consequence (Rate intensity 0–100)	D Dispute (Rate certainty 0–100)	E Effect Change (Rerate certainty in belief and intensity of urge 0–100 in Columns B and C)
Sunday 11:30 pm	I have some downtime, late at night, no plans with anyone, start to think about how fire would look in the nighttime, start to notice excitement	Fire-setting will lead to excitement and will be fun and I will not cause any damage/harm. Rating = 90 Revised rating = 25	I will have fun and no one will get hurt and nothing will get damaged. Rating = 90 Revised rating = 40	I do experience excitement and a rush of adrenaline when I think about setting a fire, when planning it, and when engaged in the act of fire-setting. I never consider the negative consequences of fire setting until after the fact. The elated mood quickly fades each time I do it. I can increase excitement again by imagining fires set in the past. I notice that I spend a lot of time thinking about fire, use up most of my free time thinking about fires, researching ways to set fires, and listening to police scanners. I have had several fires get out of control, burned garage down, set field of grass on fire, and I have been caught in the past. I have burned my hands, lost hair on my body and had to make excuses to medical personnel, friends, and coworkers. I used to have other hobbies that were healthy and that could be exciting, the benefits lasted longer (e.g., mountain biking, rock climbing), were not illegal, and I did not cause anyone harm. Although fire-setting is exciting, the thrill does not last and I risk more harm to self and others each time I do it. I think about it and spend so much time on this habit, maybe it is not as fun and exciting as I thought. Rating = 80	After considering the dispute, I would rerate how certain I was in the initial belief, as well as the intensity of my urge to start a fire.

Figure 7.4

Sample ABC Log for PY Client

clients must not have access to money for a period of time or, at the very least, have a very specific plan for how money will be managed differently. KM and PY clients will have to restrict their access to triggering events, and all clients will need loved ones to help them in managing the impulsive behavior.

It has been our experience that it will be a combination of all the strategies introduced in the CBT-ICD program that will prove to be effective in managing impulsive behaviors. Clients will also respond differently, and may prefer one intervention over another. For example, many clients struggle with, or can be resistant to, journaling their beliefs and taking the time to dispute them. You may wish to use an analogy of taking prescribed medication when explaining the effectiveness of therapy in managing symptoms.

> *Using the cognitive intervention when it counts (e.g., when your urge is active), is the equivalent of you taking your prescribed medication. We would not expect symptoms to change if you did not take your medication consistently, as prescribed. In terms of the therapy, it will take consistent, regular practice in using the cognitive intervention in order to observe an impact on symptom management. If you practice the therapy intermittently, when you think of it, or take your medication only when you think of it, we would not expect your symptoms to change because you are not using the intervention as prescribed.*

Homework

✎ Instruct the client to continue completing the Daily ICD Behavior Diary in Chapter 2 of the workbook. The client may make photocopies as necessary.

✎ Encourage the client to continue implementing healthy behaviors to combat the ICD triggers identified on the Controlling ICD Triggers Form in Chapter 4 of the workbook. Healthy coping strategies include engaging in leisure activities and utilizing the problem-solving method introduced in Session 3.

✎ If the client's peak urge rating had not decreased by 50% or greater in the past week, then have the client continue practicing imaginal exposure four times daily, with two consecutive repetitions in the morning and two in the evening, and record urge ratings on the Imaginal Exposure Rating Form in Chapter 5 of the workbook. Client's that report a reduction in peak urge rating or the imaginal exposure will then use the recording as needed.

✎ Instruct the client to complete the ABC Log and Disputing Impulsive Beliefs form whenever he or she experiences an urge to engage in impulsive behaviors. These forms can be used to evaluate past episodes of the impulsive behavior if there is no occurrence of the impulsive behavior between sessions.

For the PG or CB client:

✎ Have the client develop a budget based upon the three weeks of monitoring spending, using the Financial Budget form in Chapter 3 of the workbook.

Chapter 8

Session 6: Relapse Prevention

(Corresponds to Chapter 7 of the workbook)

Materials Needed

■ Planning for Future Triggers form

Session Outline

■ Review past week and homework

■ Introduce and discuss relapse prevention strategies

Past Week and Homework Review

Review the client's Daily ICD Behavior Diary entries from the preceding week. Check to make sure that the client continued to practice managing ICD triggers by implementing healthy behaviors. Also check that the client has continued to practice imaginal exposure until intensity of urges has decreased by at least 50%. Review the client's completed ABC Logs and Disputing Impulsive Beliefs forms.

Reevaluation

Review progress to date and use the DSM-IV-TR to determine if the client still meets criteria for the ICD initially diagnosed. Also, assess the ICD behavior with a severity rating scale to determine how much improvement has been made since the initial assessment. This final session includes a review of the risks of relapse, the nature of relapse, and techniques to avoid it. Detailed information for the client is provided in Chapter 7 of the workbook.

Future Triggers

Clients must be prepared for future triggers or stressors that may elicit an urge and subsequently put them at risk for engaging in impulsive behaviors. It is helpful to list out future ICD triggers and healthy behaviors clients can employ to prevent impulsive behaviors. Work together with the client to complete the Planning for Future Triggers form in Chapter 7 of the workbook.

Planning for the Future

Stress to the client the importance of "ongoing practice" of the skills learned in therapy. Encourage the client to continue practicing the following:

- Daily self-monitoring of urges and any impulsive behaviors.

- ICD trigger management.

- Financial management. PG and CB clients will continue to use a financial budget and adhere to a long-term plan of paying down debt. You can also suggest the client seek the services of a financial planner for long-term support and expertise in managing debt.

- Use the ABC Log and Disputing Impulsive Beliefs form whenever experiencing an urge. Clients should continue to use these forms until there is a change in their thinking, such that the objective evidence against acting impulsively becomes more automatic and accessible when an urge is experienced. It is helpful for clients to periodically review previously completed ABC Logs to observe how their thinking has changed over time since the beginning of therapy. Reviewing past thinking errors is another opportunity for developing insight and for reinforcing healthy habits.

- Healthy behaviors development. Clients will continue to plan for and implement regular leisure activities. It is important for you to review each client's progress to date with leisure skill development. A lack of a realistic plan and/or follow-through will likely be a significant risk factor for relapse. If the client has shown limited progress in this area, you may need to make efforts to find support for the client. For example, a family member, friend, or significant other may need to be involved to keep the client accountable. These concerns can be addressed in the family session as well, in order to stress the critical importance of healthy leisure activities to the client's ongoing abstinence from the impulsive behavior targeted in treatment. At this point in the treatment, you can also assist the client in planning for ongoing experimentation with different hobbies or activities, or at the very least, increasing the extent of the client's involvement in an existing activity. For example, once the client completes a community education class in beginning photography, plan for more advanced classes or investigate photography groups.

- Imaginal exposure. Clients should practice imaginal exposure as needed. If a CB or KM client is aware that she will be in a store where she has previously engaged in impulsive behaviors, listening to the exposure tape ahead of time may be helpful in reminding her of the consequences of her behavior. It has been our experience that certain clients are less inclined to write down and challenge their impulsive beliefs. Under these circumstances, such clients may be more apt to listen to the tape, because it takes less effort on their part. The exposure tape will cease to elicit an urge after several repetitions, but can be a useful reminder of negative consequences as well as healthy coping behaviors.

Chapter 9   *Session 7: Family Involvement (Optional)*

(Corresponds to Chapter 8 of the workbook)

This session may be added onto a previous session (after meeting with the client alone), or added on at the very end of treatment. It is important, however, that the six sessions of this program not be interrupted or delayed by this family session.

Some clients have significant family issues surrounding their ICD. In those cases, the client and family may be referred to family counseling after the CBT therapy, or simultaneously with this treatment. This session is seen as an initial means of addressing these issues, but in no way should substitute for more in-depth family therapy when it is warranted.

The family session involves three distinct parts:

1. Explaining the therapy to the family members so they are aware of what the client has been, or is going to be, doing.

2. Allowing the client to inform the family members about his or her impulsive behavior in a safe, neutral setting.

3. Assessing what the family members may need to help them better cope with this problem.

Education about ICDs and This Program

You may revisit many of the concepts from Session 1 at this point. Inform the family members about the disease model of impulsive behaviors, and the goals of CBT in changing the brain. Drawing parallels to diabetes or alcoholism are often helpful, as they allow the family members to understand that ICDs are a biological problem (for a review of this topic, please see Grant, Brewer, & Potenza, 2006).

Family members may report differing concerns based on the type of ICD. Family members of PG and CB clients may often have great anger toward the client due to the financial problems, lying, and manipulation that is symptomatic/characteristic of the ICD. Family members may misperceive the discussion about the biology of the ICD as an "excuse" for the client. It is important to stress that although there are strong biological factors underlying the ICD, the client is in control of whether he seeks treatment and keeps working on the therapy. This allows both the client and the family to understand that although the *illness* may be beyond the client's control, the *choice* to go through treatment isn't.

Family members may also want to know about the genetics or heritability of the ICD. They may be worried about their children or other family members. It is important to give them the facts. Education about PG can include: evidence of genetic links between pathological gambling and alcoholism, as well as between pathological gambling and depression (at least in men). You should also stress that although there are genetic links within families, genetics plays only a small part in the development of an ICD. Environmental issues, developmental processes, and unknown factors also account for the disorders. The family should be aware that other family members may develop this problem, but that it is not the client's "fault" if his children or others struggle with impulsive behaviors. Family members should be disabused of the notion that the client's illness is any sort of "infection" within the family. Family members should also be informed that they did not cause this illness, and do not have to make up for their guilt by taking care of all the problems resulting from the impulsive behavior.

Debt-Related Concerns for PG and CB

Family members may feel that they need to "rescue" the PG or CB client financially, either because they feel guilty (often felt by parents of the client), or because they worry about the client. The family members should be informed that the client is working on, or will be working on, payment plans, and that "bailing him out" is generally not a good idea.

Family members may often feel that they are "held hostage" by the debt—the client keeps telling them that they have to help, or something bad will happen. The client needs to be honest with the family about the debt, and about any repercussions relating to that debt. The family members need to be informed that they can help by working with the client to maintain the new budget.

The client and family should also be informed that the payment plan will prioritize the family. That is, when paying off debts, the client must first pay off household debt before addressing his or her own private debts. This stresses the idea that the welfare of the family comes first.

The psychological impact of ICDs within the family is often quite severe. Family members may need referrals to their own therapists, independent of any possible continued family therapy. Having some referrals to mental health professionals aware of the effects of the ICD on family members would be helpful for the family members.

Suggestions for Family Member Support

The family session provides a safe setting for the client to discuss his or her impulse control problems. Family members can be important allies in managing the symptoms of the ICD. The family session provides an opportunity for the client to discuss the extent of his impulsive behavior, the reality of the resulting problems, and what types of plans or other solutions have been put in place to deal with the problems.

Specific ways in which family members may help with the therapy:

1. Family members may be told how they can help remove or reduce the client's triggers for impulsive behaviors. For example, if a trigger is feeling lonely on Friday night, the family can start planning events with the client on Friday nights. For the first several months and up to the first year post-treatment, the client should have limited downtime. Free time should be spent on leisure skill development, repairing relationships and seeking new healthy relationships, and following through with plans to manage debt and other recurring problems caused by the ICD.

2. Family members may want to continue to work with the PG or CB client on debt. If feeling overwhelmed by debt is a trigger to shop or gamble, then regular meetings with the family to discuss bills may alleviate the catastrophic thinking and avoidance surrounding debt.

3. Family members may be elicited to help with developing or participating in new, healthier behaviors. If the client wants to start exercising instead of engaging in the impulsive behavior, family members may work out schedules with the client when they are available to join him for exercise.

4. Family members should be informed about the warning signs of relapse. They can then remind the client about his goals, and praise him when he's back on track. The therapist and client can share information with family members gathered over the course of treatment. Family members should be aware of internal and external triggers. The client can make a commitment to contact family members when feeling at risk of acting out the impulsive behavior. The family will need help and preparation in terms of the best way to respond when the client seeks out their help. The client's efforts to reach out for help need to be reinforced, and not be used as an opportunity for family members to be critical. The client and family members can have access to a list of ideas for dealing with the urge, so the focus is on problem-solving and not rehashing the past.

Helping Family Members Cope

Assess what the family members may need to cope with the client's impulsive behavior. Family members often have significant guilt and anger concerning a client's ICD. They often feel cheated, lied to, or manipulated, and feel as if they do not "know" the client. They are also very often worried about the client's welfare and in some cases, feel they have little to offer except money (i.e., the "bail out").

Family members often find that attending support groups can be helpful. Visiting with other people with similar problems, as well as other family members, can help to normalize the impulsive behavior for family members and clients. Share the following suggestions with family members for support:

- Gamblers Anonymous and/or Gam-Anon meetings can be helpful for family and friends of the PG client.

- Support groups (online or in person) can be helpful for both the client and her family. Search the Internet for ICD support groups.

- Family and/or couples therapy can be helpful for family members of the client, particularly the client's spouse or partner.

Appendix of Assessment Measures

Minnesota Impulsive Disorders Interview (MIDI)

Copyright © 2008 by Jon E. Grant

General Information

1. (Check) _____ Male _____ Female

2. (Check) _____ White _____ African-American

   _____ Hispanic _____ Asian-American

   _____ Native-American _____ Other

3. How old are you? _____ (years)

4. What do you do for a living? _____

5. What is your sexual orientation / gender identity?

   _____ heterosexual _____ bisexual

   _____ gay _____ transgender

6. What is your marital status?

   _____ Single

   _____ Married

   _____ Separated

   _____ Divorced

   _____ Widowed

7a. Do you have children?   Y   N

   7b. (if yes) How many children do you have? _____

   7c. (if yes) How old are they? _____

8a. How many years of school have you completed? _____

   8b. (if more than high school) What is the highest degree that you have obtained? _____

9. What is your approximate yearly household income? _____

1a. Do you or others think that you have a problem with buying things too often, or with spending too much money?   Y   N

   1b. (if yes) Why? _____

      _____

2a. Do you ever experience an irresistible urge or uncontrollable need to buy things or mounting tension that can only be relieved by buying?   Y   N

   2b. (if yes) Do these urges or thoughts about buying seem to be forced into your thinking or intrusive?   Y   N

   2c. (if yes) Do you attempt to resist these urges or thoughts?   Y   N

3a. Is buying followed by release of tension or a sense of gratification, even if only for the moment?   Y   N

4a. Has problem buying led to social, marital, family, financial, or work problems, or caused you to experience significant distress?   Y   N

   4b. (if yes) In which of these areas has there been a problem?

      Social   _____

      Marital   _____

      Family   _____

      Financial   _____

      Work   _____

      Personal distress   _____

      Other (specify)   _____

   4c. (if yes) How has buying affected these areas?

      _____

      _____

      _____

(If yes to Questions 1 and 4, go to <u>Structured Clinical Interview for</u> <u>Compulsive Buying</u>; if no to Question 1 or 4, end module.)

Kleptomania

1a. Have you ever stolen anything?   Y   N (if no, skip to next module)

   1b. (if yes) When did this occur?

   _____

   1c. (if yes) What did you steal?

   _____

   1d. (if yes) Do you currently steal?   Y   N

   (if yes) Please describe your current pattern of stealing:

   _____

   _____

1e. (Subject demonstrates a recurrent pattern of theft not limited to a few isolated events)   Y   N (if no, end module)

1f. Some people steal for their own personal use, or for the value things might bring in selling or trading them. Others steal for no obvious reason to others, or even to themselves, with stealing seeming senseless or impulsive. Why do you steal?

   _____

   _____

   _____

1g. What percent of your stealing is for your own use, for sale or trade, and for no apparent reason?

   Steals for monetary value   _____%

   Steals for personal use   _____%

   Steals objects not necessary for
   personal use nor for monetary value   _____%

2a. Do you experience an irresistible urge or uncontrollable need to steal things, or mounting tension that can only be relieved by stealing?   Y   N

    2b. (if yes) Do these urges or thoughts about stealing seem to be forced into your thinking or intrusive?   Y   N

    2c. (if yes) Do you attempt to resist these urges or thoughts?   Y   N

3a. Is stealing followed by release of tension or a sense of gratification, even if only for the moment?   Y   N

4a. Has stealing led to social, marital, family, financial, or work problems, or caused you personal distress?   Y   N

    4b. (if yes) In which of these areas has there been a problem?

Social	_____
Marital	_____
Family	_____
Financial	_____
Work	_____
Personal distress	_____
Other (specify)	_____

    4c. (if yes) How has stealing affected these areas?

_____

_____

_____

1. Have you ever pulled out scalp, eyelash, eyebrow, pubic or any other body hair other than for cosmetic reasons? (e.g., eyebrow plucking, pubic hair plucking for swimsuits, gray hair removal, facial hair removal)   Y   N (if no, skip to next module)

2. From the following list, please indicate which hair sites you have ever pulled from. (Check only those not pulled exclusively for cosmetic reasons; check even if subject indicates that no visible loss has been evident.)

   scalp _____

   lashes _____

   brows _____

   pubic _____

   beard _____

   mustache _____

   legs _____

   arms _____

   axillary _____

   chest _____

   abdomen _____

3. Has hair-pulling ever resulted in visible hair loss such as hair thinning, bald patches or, in the case of eyelashes, gaps along the eyelid?   Y   N (if no, end module)

4a. Do you ever experience a mounting or building tension or urge to pull hair prior to pulling hair from any site?   Y   N

   4b. (if yes) Is this different from a more general tension or anxiety that might be attributable to stressors at the time?   Y   N

5. Do you experience tension relief after pulling out hair, even if only momentarily?   Y   N

6. Do you experience a sense of pleasure or gratification after pulling out hair, even if only momentarily?   Y   N

Intermittent Explosive Disorder

The following includes questions about assaultiveness. Because the law requires me to report to the authorities threat of physical harm to others and child abuse, I strongly recommend that you not supply any more detail to questions other than that asked of you, and that you answer all yes/no questions with a yes or no response only. By following these guidelines, none of your answers will be reportable. You may choose not to answer any or all of these questions.

1a. Have you ever lost control and assaulted someone or destroyed property?   Y   N

   1b. (if yes) Has this happened on several occasions?   Y   N

   1c. (if yes) Did you cause serious injury or destruction of property during these episodes?   Y   N

   1d. Did you or others feel that these episodes were grossly out of proportion to the situation?   Y   N

   1e. Are these episodes unlike you?   Y   N

   1f. Are these episodes always associated with using alcohol or other psychoactive drugs?   Y   N

   1g. At what age did you first experience this loss of control?

2. Are you often on the edge of losing control?   Y   N

Pyromania

1a. Have you deliberately or purposefully set a fire on more than one
occasion?   Y   N (if no, skip to next module)
(if yes) Have more than one of these fires:

1b. not been set for monetary gain?   Y   N

1c. not been to conceal criminal activity?   Y   N

1d. not been out of anger or vengeance?   Y   N

1e. not been to improve your living circumstances?   Y   N

(Note: Hallucinations, delusions not addressed in this module)

2. Have you experienced any kind of urge or mounting tension prior
to setting a fire?   Y   N

3. Have certain mood changes made you feel like you had to set
a fire?   Y   N

4. Are you fascinated with, interested in, curious about or attracted
to fire, situations in which fires occur, things used to set fires, or
the consequences of fires?   Y   N

5. Do you experience pleasure, gratification, or relief when setting
fires, watching fires, or being involved with the aftermath of
fires?   Y   N

Pathological Gambling

1. Do you gamble?   Y   N (if no, skip to next module)

2. Do you or others think that you have ever had a problem with
gambling?   Y   N

3. Have you ever felt guilty about the way you gamble, or what
happens when you gamble?   Y   N

4. Have you often been preoccupied with gambling or obtaining
money to gamble?   Y   N

5. Have you frequently gambled larger amounts of money, or over longer periods of time, than you intended to?   Y   N

6. Have you found that you need to increase the size or frequency of bets to obtain the same excitement?   Y   N

7. Have you felt restless or irritable when you were unable to gamble?   Y   N

8. Have you ever tried to stop gambling and had difficulty?   Y   N

9. Have you ever decreased your involvement with or quit some important social, work, or recreational activity in order to gamble?   Y   N

10. Have you ever continued to gamble despite having significant money, social, family, or occupational problems caused or exacerbated by gambling?   Y   N

11. Have you returned to gambling despite repeatedly losing money gambling, in an attempt to win back losses?   Y   N

12. Have you frequently gambled when you were expected to meet social or occupational obligations?   Y   N

Compulsive Sexual Behavior Screen

The following section includes questions about sexual behavior. The law requires us to report to the authorities acts of physical harm to others, and child abuse. We strongly recommend that you do not supply answers to the following questions if your answers indicate that your sexual activities involve threatening others, or sexual relationships with minors, which you would not want reported. If you choose to answer only the yes/no questions, none of your answers will be reportable. You may choose not to answer any or all of these questions.

1. Do you or others that you know think that you have a problem with being overly preoccupied with some aspect of your sexuality, or being overly sexually active?   Y   N

2a. Do you have repetitive sexual fantasies that you feel are out of your control or cause you distress?   Y   N

    2b. (if yes) Can you give me examples? (if yes) Please describe this: _____

    _____

    2c. (if yes) Does the (above) fantasy frequently intrude into your mind?   Y   N

    2d. (if yes) Do you try to resist thinking about this (above) fantasy?   Y   N

    2e. (if yes) When you are having the fantasy, does it cause you to feel good or bad about yourself?
    _____ Good   _____ Bad

    2f. Do you feel ashamed about having had the fantasy after the fact?   Y   N

3a. Do you have repetitive sexual urges that you feel are out of your control, or that cause you distress?   Y   N

    3b. (if yes) Can you give me examples? (if yes) Please describe this:

    _____

    _____

    3c. (if yes) Do the (above) urges frequently intrude into your mind?   Y   N

    3d. (if yes) Do you try to resist thinking about the above urges?   Y   N

    3e. (if yes) When you are having the urges, do they cause you to feel good or bad about yourself?
    _____ Good   _____ Bad

    3f. (if yes) Do you feel ashamed about having had these urges after the fact?   Y   N

4a. Do you engage in repetitive sexual behavior which you feel is out of control, or causes you distress?　Y　　N

    4b. (if yes) Can you give me examples? (if yes) Please describe this:

        _____

        _____

        _____

    4c. (if yes) Do thoughts of these behaviors frequently intrude into your mind?　Y　　N

    4d. (if yes) Do you try to resist engaging in this behavior?　Y　　N

    4e. (if yes) When you are engaged in this behavior, does it cause you to feel good or bad about yourself?
        _____ Good　　_____ Bad

    4f. Do you feel ashamed about having engaged in the behavior after the fact?　Y　　N

Background Module

1. What did your father do for a living? _____

2. What did your mother do for a living? _____

3. Would any of the following words describe you as a child? (check all that apply)

    impulsive   _____

    passive   _____

    shy   _____

    outgoing   _____

    clingy   _____

    resistant to change
    or novelty   _____

    submissive   _____

compliant _____

sensitive _____

risk-taking _____

afraid of risks _____

perfectionistic _____

moralistic _____

indecisive _____

devoted to work _____

unappreciated _____

4. Would any of the following words describe you now? (check all that apply)

impulsive _____

passive _____

shy _____

outgoing _____

clingy _____

resistant to change
or novelty _____

submissive _____

compliant _____

sensitive _____

risk-taking _____

afraid of risks _____

perfectionistic _____

moralistic _____

indecisive _____

devoted to work _____

unappreciated _____

5. Do you have any siblings?   Y   N
   (if yes, detail sex and age)

   Sex   Age   Sex   Age

   ___   ___   ___   ___

   ___   ___   ___   ___

   ___   ___   ___   ___

6a. Have you ever been physically abused?   Y   N

   6b. (if yes) At what ages did this occur? _____ years old

7a. Have you ever been sexually abused?   Y   N

   7b. (if yes) At what ages did this occur? _____ years old

Compulsive Buying

Positive screen if the subject answers "yes" to 1a, 2a, 3a, **and** 4a

Kleptomania

Positive screen if the subject answers "yes" to 1a, 2a, 3a, **and** 4a

Trichotillomania

Positive screen if the subject answers "yes" to 1, 3, 4a, 5, **and** 6

Intermittent Explosive Disorder

Positive screen if the subject answers "yes" to 1a, 1b, 1c, **and** 1d; **in addition**, the subject must answer "no" to 1f

Pyromania

Positive screen if the subject answers "yes" to 1a, 2, 3, 4, **and** 5; **in addition**, the subject must answer "no" to 1b, 1c, 1d, and 1e

Pathological Gambling

Positive screen if the subject answers "yes" to 1, **and** to at least 5 of the rest of the questions

Compulsive Sexual Behavior

Positive screen if the subject answers "yes" to 1, 2a, 3a, **or** 4a

Date:_____

SKIP IF ALREADY KNOWN

Have you ever gambled for money or other items of values?

___Yes   ___No

NOTES

If answer is yes, continue:

_____

_____

How often do you gamble now?   _____

How much money do you typically gamble?   _____

When was the last time you gambled?   _____

_____

When in your life were you gambling most? _____

How long did that period last?   _____

_____

During that time . . .   _____

    how often were you gambling?   _____

    what kind of gambling did you do?   _____

    how much did you gamble when
    you gambled?   _____

_____

During that time . . .   _____

    did your gambling cause problems
    for you?   _____

    did anyone object to your gambling?   _____

                                     _____

                                     _____

                                     _____

Proceed if there has ever been an indication of high-frequency gambling or large amounts of money gambled, or negative social, family, school, occupational, or legal consequences.

NOTE TO INTERVIEWER: Use space below each question to describe responses to each question.

For each criterion, circle one of the following four choices:

? = Inadequate information
1 = absent or false
2 = subthreshold
3 = threshold or true

A Criteria	Persistent and recurrent maladaptive gambling behavior as indicated by five or more of the 10 criteria listed below:

Let me ask you a few more questions about your gambling. We will be talking primarily about the time when you were gambling most.

NOTE TO INTERVIEWER: Change tense of questions if time of most gambling was in the past.

(The criteria are presented in a different order than appears in DSM-IV-TR.)

How often do you think about gambling? How much do you think about past gambling experiences? How often do you imagine or plan future gambling? How often do you think about getting money to gamble or pay back gambling debts? Do your thoughts about gambling get in the way of concentration on work, family or other responsibilities?	**A1.** Preoccupied with gambling (e.g., preoccupied with reliving past gambling experiences, handicapping or planning the next venture, or thinking of ways to get money with which to gamble).	? 1 2 3
At the time when you were gambling the most, what were the reasons you gambled? **If the following was not specifically stated, ask:** Did you ever gamble to … escape problems in your life? relieve uncomfortable or bad feelings or moods? How often did this happen?	**A5.** Gambles as a way of escaping? from problems or of relieving a dysphoric mood (e.g., feelings of helplessness, guilt, anxiety, depression)	? 1 2 3
In response to the previous question, you said that you gambled in order to _____ _____ Have you needed to increase the amount of money you gambled in order to get what you sought from gambling? If yes:　How large was the increase in money? If no:　Did you find that when you gambled the same amount it had much less effect than before?	**A2.** Needs to gamble with increasing amount of money in order to achieve the desired excitement. (Tolerance is defined by either of the following: (a) a need for markedly increased amounts of money wagered to achieve the desired effect sought after; (b) markedly diminished effect with continued gambling of the same amount of money.)	? 1 2 3

When you have lost money gambling, have you ever chased after your losses? In other words, have you often returned to try to get even? If no: When you have lost money, have you gambled more and more money to try and make up for losses?	**A6.** After losing money gambling, often returns another day to get even ("chasing" one's losses). (Significant losses result in acceleration of frequency and size of bets. This pattern occurs during a single gambling trip/binge for one or more days, or over a number of independent days of gambling spread over a period of time.)	? 1 2 3
Have you ever lied to anyone about gambling, such as how long you gambled, or the amount of money gambled, or that you were gambling at all? To whom did you lie? How often?	**A7.** Lies to family members, therapist, or others to conceal extent of involvement with gambling. (Exhibits pattern of lies over time in order to maintain the gambling without interference or curtailment.)	? 1 2 3
Has your gambling caused problems for you in your family, work, school or social life to the extent that you lost or risked losing something or someone important? Has gambling resulted in any other losses, such as damage or risk to your reputation, or your mental or physical health?	**A9.** Gambling has risked the loss of or resulted in the loss of a relationship, work, or educational opportunity.	? 1 2 3

Ask the following questions if further information is needed:

Have you attempted to control your gambling by cutting back or stopping? If yes: How many times? How successful have you been in trying to cut down or stop? Did you ever stop gambling entirely? If no: Did you ever want to stop or cut back? If yes: Is this something you have been worrying about?	**A3.** Repeated unsuccessful efforts to control, cut back, or stop gambling. (There is a persistent desire to control, cut down, or stop gambling, or unsuccessful efforts to do so.)	? 1 2 3

If "yes" to having tried to control, cut back or stop gambling, ask: Did you experience restlessness or irritability when you tried to cut back or stop gambling? Did you experience any other discomfort or upset when cutting back or stopping gambling, such as trouble sleeping, sweating, hands shaking, or anxiety? If "no" to the above symptoms when trying to control, cut back or stop, or "no" to having ever tried to do so, ask: Did you experience any of the signs I just listed when you wanted to gamble but the situation prevented gambling .when you had no money or there was no gambling opportunity?	**A4.** Restless or irritable when attempting to cut down or stop gambling. (Withdrawal is manifested by at least two of the following: anxiety, irritability, restlessness, sleeplessness, sweating, hand tremor.)	? 1 2 3
Have you ever asked for money or been given money from a family member or close friend to relieve a desperate financial situation caused by gambling?	**A10.** Relies on others to provide money to relieve a desperate financial situation caused by gambling. (Bailed out of a desperate financial situation by way of a gift or loan from a significant other).	? 1 2 3
Have you ever done anything illegal to get money to gamble or to pay gambling debts? For example: Have you ever passed a bad check, such as writing a check when you knew there was not enough money in the account to cover the check? Have you written checks to accounts in different banks to keep bad checks afloat ("kiting" checks)? Have you passed a check after signing or forging someone else's name on it? Have you lied about the facts when submitting an insurance claim? Have you taken money from someone or from somewhere without permission (including a family member), even if you planned to return the money?	**A8.** Committed illegal acts such as forgery, fraud, theft or embezzlement to finance gambling? (Committed illegal acts to finance gambling or to pay off pressing gambling-related loans. Acts may or may not have resulted in arrests. Includes financial acts against family members which would be crimes if committed against non-family members.)	? 1 2 3

B Criterion

NOTE TO INTERVIEWER: If this module is being used in conjunction with the SCID, refer to *Manic Episode* criteria.

If manic episode criteria not met, may rate as "gambling behavior not better accounted for by a manic episode."

If manic episode criteria met, ask the following:

Is your gambling mainly limited to the period(s) when you are feeling _____ (use own word equivalent for mania)?

Do you gamble generally only when you are

_____

(use manic symptoms acknowledged)

for example:

… sleeping only a few hours a night, yet still feeling rested?

… feeling more self confident than usual?

… experiencing thoughts racing through your head?

… having more difficulty than usual maintaining concentration or focus?)

REMINDER TO INTERVIEWER: Period of manic behavior must last for at least one week to qualify as a Manic Episode.

B. The gambling behavior is not better accounted for by a Manic Episode.

NOTE TO INTERVIEWER:
Circle 3 for gambling behavior not better accounted for by a manic episode.

(Since individuals who experience manic episodes sometimes gamble in ways that appear similar to pathological gambling, manic episodes must be ruled out as the primary cause of the diagnostic indicators of pathological gambling. However, it is possible that diagnoses of both pathological gambling and bipolar disorder may be made.)

?

1

2

3

Number of 'A' Criteria present: _____

'B' Criterion present?   Yes _____   No _____

To meet diagnostic criteria for pathological gambling, subject must meet threshold for five or more of the ten 'A' criteria <u>and</u> the one 'B' criterion.

Final determination for diagnosis of pathological gambling:

| Present | | Absent |

Yale-Brown Obsessive-Compulsive Scale Modified for Pathological Gambling (PG-YBOCS)

With kind permission from Springer Science & Business Media: *Journal of Gambling Studies,* Reliability and Validity of the Pathological Gambling Adaptation of the Yale-Brown Obsessive-Compulsive Scale (PG-YBOCS), 21(4): 431–443, 2005, Pallanti S, DeCaria CM, Grant JE, Urpe M, Hollander E.

Date of Assessment: _____

For each item, circle the number identifying the response which best characterizes the patient.

1. TIME OCCUPIED BY URGES/THOUGHTS ABOUT GAMBLING How much of your time is occupied by urges/thoughts (u/t) related to gambling and/or gambling-related activities? How frequently does this occur?	0 = None 1 = Mild (less than 1 hr/day), or occasional u/t ($\leq$ 8 x/day). 2 = Moderate (1–3 hrs/day), or frequent u/t (> 8 x/day, but most hrs/day are free of u/t) 3 = Severe (>3 = up to 8 hrs/day) or very frequent u/t (>8 x/day & occur most hrs of day). 4 = Extreme (> 8 hrs/day), or near constant u/t (too numerous to count and an hour rarely passes w/o several such u/t occurring).
2. INTERFERENCE DUE TO URGES/THOUGHTS ABOUT GAMBLING How much do your urges/thoughts (u/t) interfere with your social or work (or role) functioning? Is there anything that you don't do because of this?	0 = None 1 = Mild, slight interference with social or occupational activity but overall performance not impaired. 2 = Moderate, definite interference with social or occupational performance, but manageable. 3 = Severe, causes substantial impairment in social or occupational performance. 4 = Extreme, incapacitating.

3. DISTRESS ASSOCIATED WITH URGES/ THOUGHTS ABOUT GAMBLING How much distress do your urges/thoughts about gambling cause you? (Rate "disturbing" feeling or anxiety that seems to be triggered by these thoughts, not generalized anxiety or anxiety associated w/other symptoms).	0 = None 1 = Mild, infrequent, and not too disturbing. 2 = Moderate, frequent, & disturbing, but still manageable. 3 = Severe, very frequent, and very disturbing. 4 = Extreme, near constant, and disabling distress.
4. RESISTANCE AGAINST URGES/THOUGHTS OF GAMBLING How much of an effort do you make to resist these urges/thoughts? How often do you try to disregard them? (Only rate effort made to resist, not success or failure in actually controlling these thoughts. How much one resists the urges/thoughts may/may not correlate w/ ability to control them.)	0 = Makes effort to always resist, symptoms so minimal doesn't need to actively resist. 1 = Tries to resist most of the time. 2 = Makes some effort to resist. 3 = Yields to all such urges/ thoughts without attempting to control them, but does so with some reluctance. 4 = Completely and willingly yields to all such urges/ thoughts.
5. DEGREE OR CONTROL OVER URGES/ THOUGHTS ABOUT GAMBLING How much control do you have over urges/thoughts about gambling? How successful are you in stopping or diverting these urges/ thoughts?	0 = Complete control. 1 = Much control, usually able to stop/divert urges/ thoughts with some effort & consideration. 2 = Moderate control, sometimes able to stop/divert these urges/thoughts. 3 = Little control, rarely successful in stopping these urges/thoughts, can only divert attention with difficulty. 4 = No control, experienced as completely involuntary, rarely able to even momentarily divert urges/thoughts.

6. TIME SPENT IN ACTIVITIES RELATED TO GAMBLING How much time do you spend in activities related to gambling? (directly related to gambling itself, or activities such as negotiating financial transactions or searching for financial resources related to gambling).	0 = None 1 = Mild (spends less than 1 hr/day in these activities, or occasional involvement in these activities (≤ 8 times/day). 2 = Moderate (1–3 hrs/day) or > 8 times/day, but most hours are free of such activities. 3 = Severe (spends > 3 and up to 8 hrs/day), or very frequent involvement (> 8 times/day and activities performed most hours of the day). 4 = Extreme (spends > 8 hrs/day in these activities), or near constant involvement (too numerous to count and an hour rarely passes without engaging in several such activities).
7. INTERFERENCE DUE TO ACTIVITIES RELATED TO GAMBLING How much do the (above) activities interfere with your social/work (or role) functioning? Is there anything that you don't do because of them? (If currently not working, determine how much performance would be affected if patient were employed.)	0 = None. 1 = Mild, slight interference with social or occupational activities, but overall performance not impaired. 2 = Moderate, definite interference with social/ occupational performance, but still manageable. 3 = Severe, causes substantial impairment in social/ occupational performance. 4 = Extreme, incapacitating.
8. DISTRESS ASSOCIATED WITH BEHAVIOR RELATED TO GAMBLING How would you feel if prevented from performing these activities? (Pause) How anxious would you become?	0 = None. 1 = Mild, only slightly anxious if behavior prevented, or only slight anxiety during the behavior. 2 = Moderate, reports that anxiety would mount but remains manageable if behavior is prevented, or that anxiety increases but remains manageable during such behaviors. 3 = Severe, prominent and very disturbing increase in anxiety if behavior is interrupted, or prominent and very disturbing increase in anxiety during the behavior. 4 = Extreme, incapacitating anxiety from any intervention aimed at modifying activity, or incapacitating anxiety develops during behavior related to gambling.

9. RESISTANCE AGAINST GAMBLING How much of an effort do you make to resist these activities? (How much the patient resists behaviors may/may not correlate w/ ability to control them.)	0 = Makes an effort to always resist, or symptoms so minimal doesn't need to actively resist 1 = Tries to resist most of the time 2 = Makes some effort to resist. 3 = Yields to almost all of these behaviors without attempting to control them, but does so with some reluctance. 4 = Completely and willingly yields to all behaviors related to gambling.
10. DEGREE OF CONTROL OVER GAMBLING BEHAVIOR How strong is the drive to gamble? How much control do you have over the behaviors associated with gambling-related activities?	0 = Complete control. 1 = Much control, experiences pressure to gamble, but usually able to exercise voluntary control over it. 2 = Moderate control, strong pressure to gamble, must be carried to completion, can only delay with difficulty. 3 = Little control, very strong drive to gamble, must be carried to completion, can only delay with difficulty, 4 = No control, drive to gamble experienced as completely involuntary & overpowering, rarely able to even momentarily delay gambling activity.

Urge/Thought Subscale Score _____

Behavior Subscale Score _____

Total Score _____

Scoring:

Maximum score = 48

Extreme = over 40

Severe = 31–40

Moderate = 21–30

Mild = 8–20

The following questionnaire is aimed at evaluating gambling symptoms. Please **read** the questions **carefully** before you answer.

1) **If you had unwanted urges to gamble during the past WEEK, on average, how strong were your urges? Please circle the most appropriate number:**

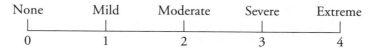

None	Mild	Moderate	Severe	Extreme
0	1	2	3	4

2) **During the past WEEK, how many times did you experience urges to gamble? Please circle the most appropriate number.**

0) None

1) Once

2) Two to three times

3) Several to many times

4) Constant or near constant

3) **During the past WEEK, how many hours (add up hours) were you preoccupied with your urges to gamble? Please circle the most appropriate number.**

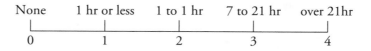

None	1 hr or less	1 to 1 hr	7 to 21 hr	over 21hr
0	1	2	3	4

4) **During the past WEEK, how much were you able to control your urges? Please circle the most appropriate number.**

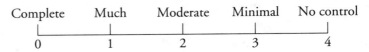

Complete	Much	Moderate	Minimal	No control
0	1	2	3	4

5) **During the past WEEK, how often did thoughts about gambling and placing bets come up? Please circle the most appropriate number.**

0) None

1) Once

2) Two to four times

3) Several to many times

4) Constantly or nearly constantly

6) **During the past WEEK, approximately how many hours (add up hours) did you spend thinking about gambling and thinking about placing bets? Please circle the most appropriate number.**

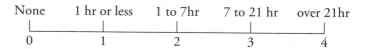

None	1 hr or less	1 to 7hr	7 to 21 hr	over 21hr
0	1	2	3	4

7) **During the past WEEK, how much were you able to control your thoughts of gambling? Please circle the most appropriate number.**

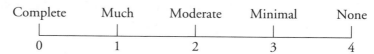

Complete	Much	Moderate	Minimal	None
0	1	2	3	4

8) **During the past WEEK, approximately how much total time did you spend gambling or on gambling related activities? Please circle the most appropriate number.**

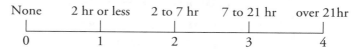

None	2 hr or less	2 to 7 hr	7 to 21 hr	over 21hr
0	1	2	3	4

9) **During the past WEEK, on average, how much anticipatory tension and/or excitement did you have <u>shortly before</u> you engaged in gambling? If you did not actually gamble, please estimate how much tension and/or excitement you believe you would have experienced, if you had gambled. Please circle the most appropriate number.**

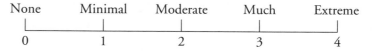

None	Minimal	Moderate	Much	Extreme
0	1	2	3	4

10) **During the past WEEK, on average, how much excitement and pleasure did you feel when you won on your bet. If you did not actually win at gambling, please estimate how much excitement and pleasure you would have experienced, if you had won. Please circle the most appropriate number.**

None	Minimal	Moderate	Much	Extreme
0	1	2	3	4

11) **During the past WEEK how much emotional distress (mental pain or anguish, shame, guilt, embarrassment) has your gambling caused you? Please circle the most appropriate number.**

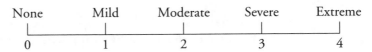

None	Mild	Moderate	Severe	Extreme
0	1	2	3	4

12) **During the past WEEK how much personal trouble (relationship, financial, legal, job, medical or health) has your gambling caused you? Please circle the most appropriate number.**

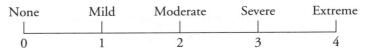

None	Mild	Moderate	Severe	Extreme
0	1	2	3	4

Reprinted from *Psychiatry Research, 166*(1), Kim SW, Grant JE, Potenza MN, Blanco C, Hollander E. The Gambling Symptom Assessment Scale (G-SAS): A reliability and validity study, pp.76–84, 2009, with permission from Elsevier.

Structured Clinical Interview for Kleptomania (SCI-K)

Date: _____

SKIP IF ALREADY KNOWN.

Have you ever stolen anything?   _____Yes _____No

NOTES

If answer is yes, continue: _____

_____

At what age did you start stealing?   _____

When in your life were you stealing most?   _____

How long did that period last?   _____

How often do you steal now?   _____

When was the last time you stole?   _____

During that time (when you were
stealing most) . . .   _____

how often were you stealing?   _____

what kind of items did you steal?   _____

what did you usually do with the items?   _____

did you have the money to buy the items?   _____

During that time . . .   _____

how did you feel right before you
stole something?   _____

how did you feel right after stealing?   _____

did you do engage in other illegal activities?   _____

if so, what kinds of illegal activities   _____

Proceed if there has ever been an indication of an inability to resist stealing.

NOTE TO INTERVIEWER: Use space below each question to describe responses to each question

For each criterion, circle one of the following four choices:

? = Inadequate information
1 = absent or false
2 = subthreshold
3 = threshold or true

Let me ask you a few more questions about your stealing. We will be talking primarily about the time when you were stealing most.

NOTE TO INTERVIEWER: Change tense of questions if time of most stealing was in the past.

Criterion
Rating

Criterion A1.	**Recurrent impulses to**	?
How often do you steal?	**steal objects**	
Why do you steal?		1
IF UNCLEAR, do you have urges or cravings to steal?		
Do you steal because you're bored or depressed?		2
Do you steal because friends or family steal?		
Do you have urges or temptations to steal, even when you don't steal?		3
How often do you have a drive, urge, or temptation to steal?		
Do you feel that your stealing is out of control?		

Criterion A2.	Recurrent failure to resist impulses	?
When you have a temptation, drive or urge to steal, have you tried not to steal?		1
(If yes) How often do you try? ... most of the time? ... some of the time? ... rarely?		2
How often were you successful in stopping yourself? ... most of the time? ... some of the time? ... rarely?		3
Do you generally feel unable to stop yourself from stealing when you have the temptation, urge or drive to steal?		

Criterion A3.	Steals items not needed for personal use or for their monetary value	?
What types of items do you steal?		1
Do you need the items you steal?		
Could you afford to buy the items instead of stealing them?		2
What do you do with the items you steal? ... sell them for money? ... return them to the store for other items or for money? ... give them away in exchange for something else?		3
Do you sometimes steal items that seem silly or nonsensical to you to steal?		
Do you ever steal the same items, or types of items, over and over again?		

Criterion B.	Increasing sense of tension immediately before committing the theft	?
I now want to ask you about		
the period (this may be minutes or hours) just before you steal		
How do you feel right before you steal something? ... Is this different from how you usually feel?		1
Does the way you feel before stealing get better or worse if you ... delay stealing, ... are prevented from stealing, or ... don't steal anything?		2
		3
Does the feeling you have before stealing go away if you steal?		

Criterion C.	**Pleasure, gratification, or relief at the time of committing the theft**	?
I now want to ask you about the very moment when you're stealing something		
How do you feel when you're stealing something? … Do you feel exhilarated/is there a "rush"? … Do you feel powerful? … Do you feel happy or satisfied?		1 2
Does the act of stealing change the way you feel?		
Does the act of stealing help to calm you down or make you feel less tense?		3
Criterion D1.	**The stealing is not committed to express anger or vengeance**	?
Have you ever stolen when you were feeling angry?		
… **If you stole from an individual,** were you angry at the person you stole from? **or,**		1
were you trying to "get even" for yourself or someone close to you?		2
… **If you stole from a store,** were you upset about the way someone in the store had treated you or treated someone close to you? **or,**		3
did you feel you deserved what you stole because the store has so much money and you don't **or,**		
were you stealing for a social or political reason aimed against that particular store?		
(If yes):		
Is this the reason (use subject's reason) that you *usually* steal?		

Criterion D2.	**Stealing is not committed in response to a delusion or a hallucination**	
I'd like to ask you about unusual experiences….		?
Have you ever stolen because you felt a store or person was going out of their way to hurt you or give you a hard time?		1
Have you stolen because you felt you were especially important in some way, or had special powers?		2
Have you stolen because someone or something outside yourself was controlling your actions against your will?		3
Have you stolen because you heard voices of people telling you to steal, even when no one was with you?		
(If yes):		
Is this the reason (use subject's reason) that you *usually* steal?		

Exclusion Criteria:

NOTE TO INTERVIEWER: if this module is being used in conjunction with the SCID, refer to Manic Episode criteria.

If Manic Episode criteria are not met, you may rate as "stealing behavior not better accounted for by a manic episode."

If Manic Episode criteria are met, ask the following:
Is your stealing mainly limited to the period(s) when you are feeling _____
(use subject's own
word(s) for mania)?

Do you steal generally only when you are

_____

(use manic symptoms acknowledged)
for example:
… sleeping only a few hours a night yet still feeling rested?
… feeling more self confident than usual?
… experiencing thoughts racing through your head?
… having more difficulty than usual maintaining concentration or focus?)

REMINDER TO INTERVIEWER: Period of manic behavior must last for at least one week to qualify as a Manic Episode.

The stealing behavior is not better accounted for by a Manic Episode. ? 1

NOTE TO INTERVIEWER

Circle 3 for stealing behavior __not__ better accounted for by a manic episode 2 3

(Since individuals who experience manic episodes sometimes steal in ways that appear similar to kleptomania, manic episodes must be ruled out as the primary cause of the diagnostic indicators of kleptomania. However, diagnoses of both kleptomania and Bipolar Disorder may be made when both are present independently.)

If this module is being used in conjunction with the SCID-II, refer to Antisocial Personality Disorder criteria.

If Antisocial Personality Disorder criteria are not met, you may rate as "stealing behavior not better accounted for by antisocial personality disorder."

The stealing behavior is not better accounted for by antisocial personality disorder ? 1 2

Circle 3 for stealing behavior __not__ better accounted for by antisocial personality disorder. 3

**If Antisocial Personality Disorder
criteria not asked,**
Before you were 15 years old, did you
… initiate physical fights?
… bully others?
… use weapons?
… act physically cruel to others?
… act physically cruel to animals?
… force someone into sexual activity?
… set fires?
… deliberately destroy property?
… break into someone else's car or home?
… run away from home or stay out all night?

If Antisocial Personality Disorder
criteria are met, ask the following:
Is your stealing mainly limited to items you don't
need or could afford to buy?

Is your stealing generally due to having
a drive, temptation, or urge to steal?

(Since individuals who suffer from
antisocial personality disorder sometimes
steal in ways that appear similar to
kleptomania, antisocial personality
disorder must be ruled out as the primary
cause of the diagnostic indicators of
kleptomania.

However, diagnoses of both kleptomania
and antisocial personality disorder may
be made if they are present
independently)

**To meet diagnostic criteria for kleptomania, the subject must meet
threshold for <u>all</u> criteria, and must not meet exclusion criteria.**

Final determination for diagnosis of kleptomania:

| **Present** | **Absent** |

Yale-Brown Obsessive-Compulsive Scale modified for Kleptomania

Date of Assessment: _____

For each item, circle the number identifying the response which best characterizes the patient.	
1. TIME OCCUPIED BY URGES/THOUGHTS ABOUT STEALING How much of your time is occupied by urges/thoughts (u/t) related to stealing and/or stealing-related activities? How frequently does this occur?	0 = None 1 = Mild (less than 1 hr/day), or occasional u/t ($\leq$ 8 x/day). 2 = Moderate (1-3 hrs/day), or frequent u/t (> 8 x/day, but most hrs/day are free of u/t) 3 = Severe (>3 = up to 8 hrs/day) or very frequent u/t (>8 x/day & occur most hrs of day). 4 = Extreme (> 8 hrs/day), or near constant u/t (too numerous to count and an hour rarely passes w/o several such u/t occurring).
2. INTERFERENCE DUE TO URGES/THOUGHTS ABOUT STEALING How much do your urges/thoughts interfere with your social or work (or role) functioning? Is there anything that you don't do because of this? (If not currently working, determine how much performance would be affected if employed).	0 = None 1 = Mild, slight interference with social or occupational activity but overall performance not impaired. 2 = Moderate, definite interference with social or occupational performance, but manageable. 3 = Severe, causes substantial impairment in social or occupational performance. 4 = Extreme, incapacitating.
3. DISTRESS ASSOCIATED WITH URGES/THOUGHTS ABOUT STEALING How much distress do your urges/thoughts about stealing cause you? (Rate "disturbing" feeling or anxiety that seems to be triggered by these thoughts, not generalized anxiety or anxiety associated w/other symptoms).	0 = None 1 = Mild, infrequent, and not too disturbing. 2 = Moderate, frequent, & disturbing, but still manageable. 3 = Severe, very frequent, and very disturbing. 4 = Extreme, near constant, and disabling distress.

4. RESISTANCE AGAINST URGES/THOUGHTS OF STEALING How much of an effort do you make to resist these urges/thoughts? How often do you try to disregard them? (Only rate effort made to resist, not success or failure in actually controlling these thoughts. How much one resists the urges/thoughts may/may not correlate w/ ability to control them.)	0 = Makes effort to always resist, symptoms so minimal doesn't need to actively resist. 1 = Tries to resist most of the time. 2 = Makes some effort to resist. 3 = Yields to all such urges/thoughts without attempting to control them, but does so with some reluctance. 4 = Completely and willingly yields to all such urges/thoughts.
5. DEGREE OR CONTROL OVER URGES/THOUGHTS ABOUT STEALING How much control do you have over urges/thoughts about stealing? How successful are you in stopping or diverting these urges/thoughts?	0 = Complete control. 1 = Much control, usually able to stop/divert urges/thoughts with some effort & consideration. 2 = Moderate control, sometimes able to stop/divert these urges/thoughts. 3 = Little control, rarely successful in stopping these urges/thoughts, can only divert attention with difficulty. 4 = No control, experienced as completely involuntary, rarely able to even momentarily divert urges/thoughts.
6. TIME SPENT IN ACTIVITIES RELATED TO STEALING How much time do you spend in activities related to stealing? (Directly related to stealing itself, or activities such as negotiating financial transactions or searching for financial resources related to stealing).	0 = None 1 = Mild (spends less than 1 hr/day in these activities, or occasional involvement in these activities ($\leq$ 8 times/day). 2 = Moderate (1-3 hrs/day) or > 8 times/day, but most hours are free of such activities. 3 = Severe (spends > 3 and up to 8 hrs/day), or very frequent involvement (> 8 times/day and activities performed most hours of the day). 4 = Extreme (spends > 8 hrs/day in these activities), or near constant involvement (too numerous to count and an hour rarely passes without engaging in several such activities).

7. INTERFERENCE DUE TO ACTIVITIES RELATED TO STEALING How much do the (above) activities interfere with you social/work (or role) functioning? Is there anything that you don't do because of them? (If currently not working, determine how much performance would be affected if patient were employed.)	0 = None. 1 = Mild, slight interference with social or occupational activities, but overall performance not impaired. 2 = Moderate, definite interference with social/occupational performance, but still manageable. 3 = Severe, causes substantial impairment in social/ occupational performance. 4 = Extreme, incapacitating.
8. DISTRESS ASSOCIATED WITH BEHAVIOR RELATED TO STEALING How would you feel if prevented from performing these activities? (Pause) How anxious would you become?	0 = None. 1 = Mild, only slightly anxious if behavior prevented, or only slight anxiety during the behavior. 2 = Moderate, reports that anxiety would mount but remains manageable if behavior is prevented, or that anxiety increases but remains manageable during such behaviors. 3 = Severe, prominent and very disturbing increase in anxiety if behavior is interrupted, or prominent and very disturbing increase in anxiety during the behavior. 4 = Extreme, incapacitating anxiety from any intervention aimed at modifying activity, or incapacitating anxiety develops during behavior related to stealing.
9. RESISTANCE AGAINST STEALING How much of an effort do you make to resist these activities? (How much the patient resists behaviors may/ may not correlate w/ability to control them.)	0 = Makes an effort to always resist, or symptoms so minimal doesn't need to actively resist 1 = Tries to resist most of the time 2 = Makes some effort to resist. 3 = Yields to almost all of these behaviors without attempting to control them, but does so with some reluctance. 4 = Completely and willingly yields to all behaviors related to stealing.

10. DEGREE OF CONTROL OVER STEALING BEHAVIOR How strong is the drive to steal? How much control do you have over the behaviors associated with stealing-related activities?	0 = Complete control. 1 = Much control, experiences pressure to steal, but usually able to exercise voluntary control over it. 2 = Moderate control, strong pressure to steal, must be carried to completion, can only delay with difficulty. 3 = Little control, very strong drive to steal, must be carried to completion, can only delay with difficulty, 4 = No control, drive to steal experienced as completely involuntary & overpowering, rarely able to even momentarily delay stealing activity

Urge/Thought Subscale Score _____

Behavior Subscale Score _____

Total Score _____

The following questions are aimed at evaluating kleptomania symptoms. Please **read** the questions **carefully** before you answer.

1) **If you had urges to steal during the past WEEK, on average, how strong were your urges? Please circle the most appropriate number:**

None	Mild	Moderate	Severe	Extreme
0	1	2	3	4

2) **During the past WEEK, how many times did you experience urges to steal? Please circle the most appropriate number.**

0) None

1) Once

2) Two to four times

3) Several to many times

4) Constantly or nearly constantly

3) **During the past WEEK, how many hours (add up hours) were you preoccupied with your urges to steal? Please circle the most appropriate number.**

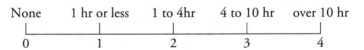

None	1 hr or less	1 to 4hr	4 to 10 hr	over 10 hr
0	1	2	3	4

4) **During the past WEEK, how much were you able to control your urges? Please circle the most appropriate number.**

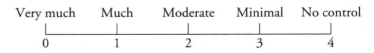

Very much	Much	Moderate	Minimal	No control
0	1	2	3	4

5) **During the past WEEK, how often did thoughts about stealing come up? Please circle the most appropriate number.**

0) None

1) Once

2) Two to four times

3) Several to many times

4) Constantly or nearly constantly

6) **During the past WEEK, approximately how many hours (add up hours) did you spend thinking about stealing? Please circle the most appropriate number.**

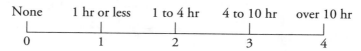

7) **During the past WEEK, how much were you able to control your thoughts of stealing? Please circle the most appropriate number.**

Very much	Much	Moderate	Minimal	None
0	1	2	3	4

8) **During the past WEEK, on average, how much tension or excitement did you have <u>shortly before</u> you committed a theft? If you did not actually steal anything, please estimate how much anticipatory tension or excitement you believe you would have experienced, if you had committed a theft. Please circle the most appropriate number.**

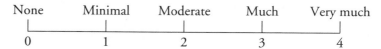

None	Minimal	Moderate	Much	Very much
0	1	2	3	4

9) **During the past WEEK, on average, how much excitement and pleasure did you feel when you successfully committed a theft? If you did not actually steal, please estimate how much excitement and pleasure you believe you would have experienced if you had committed a theft. Please circle the most appropriate number.**

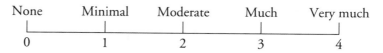

None	Minimal	Moderate	Much	Very much
0	1	2	3	4

10) **During the past WEEK, how much emotional distress (mental pain or anguish, shame, guilt, embarrassment) has your stealing caused you? Circle the most appropriate number.**

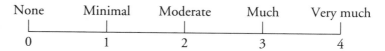

None	Minimal	Moderate	Much	Very much
0	1	2	3	4

11) During the past WEEK, how much personal trouble (relationship, financial, legal, job, medical or health) has your stealing caused you? Please circle the most appropriate number.

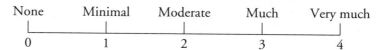

None	Minimal	Moderate	Much	Very much
0	1	2	3	4

Structured Clinical Interview for Compulsive Buying

NOTE TO INTERVIEWER: Use space below each question to describe responses to each question.

For each criterion, circle one of the following four choices:

> ? = Inadequate information
>
> 1 = absent or false
>
> 2 = subthreshold
>
> 3 = threshold or true

Criterion A. I'd now like to ask you some more questions about when you were shopping/buying the most, or about a time when shopping/buying caused the most problems **MUST MEET EITHER SUB-CRITERION A(1) OR A(2)**	**Persistent and recurrent maladaptive behavior as a result of excessive buying/shopping as indicated by <u>at least one</u> of the following:**
Sub-Criterion A(1) Did you often think about shopping/buying? Do you have difficulty controlling your shopping/buying?	**Frequent preoccupation with buying or impulses to buy that is/are experienced as irresistible, intrusive, and/or senseless.** ? 1 2 3
Sub-Criterion A(2) Did you often find that when you went shopping you ended up doing so for longer periods of time than you were planning to, or spending much more money than you intended?	**Frequent buying of more than can be afforded, frequent buying of items that are not needed, or shopping for longer periods of time than intended.** ? 1 2 3
Criterion B. Has your shopping/buying caused serious problems for you with your family or friends, with your (spouse/partner), or with work or school?	**The buying preoccupations, impulses, or behaviors cause marked distress, are time-consuming, significantly interfere with social or occupational functioning, or result in financial problems (e.g., indebtedness or bankruptcy).** ? 1 2 3

Criterion C (Exclusionary Criteria).

NOTE TO INTERVIEWER: if this module is being used in conjunction with the SCID, refer to Manic Episode criteria.

If Manic Episode criteria are <u>not</u> met, you may rate as "buying behavior not better accounted for by a manic episode."

If Manic Episode criteria are met, ask the following:

Is your buying mainly limited to the period(s) when you are feeling _____ (use subject's own word(s) for mania)?

Does your shopping or buying generally occur only when you are _____ (use manic symptoms acknowledged) for example:

… sleeping only a few hours a night yet still feeling rested?

… feeling more self confident than usual?

… experiencing thoughts racing through your head?

… having more difficulty than usual maintaining concentration or focus?)

REMINDER TO INTERVIEWER: Period of manic behavior must last for at least one week to qualify as a Manic Episode.

The excessive shopping/buying behavior does not occur exclusively during periods of hypomania or mania
(*Circle "3" for shopping/buying behavior <u>not</u> better accounted for by hypomania or mania*).

1   3

To meet diagnostic criteria for Compulsive Buying, the subject must meet threshold for A(1) OR A(2) AND B criteria, and must not meet exclusion (Criterion C) criteria.

Final determination for diagnosis of Compulsive Buying:

| Present | | Absent |

Date of Assessment: _____

For each item, circle the number identifying the response which best characterizes the patient.	
1. TIME OCCUPIED BY URGES/THOUGHTS ABOUT SHOPPING How much of your time is occupied by urges/thoughts about shopping?	0 = None 1 = Mild, <1 h / day or occasional intrusion 2 = Moderate, 1–3 h / day, or frequent intrusion 3 = Severe, >3 and up to 8 hrs/day) or very frequent intrusion 4 = Extreme, >8 hrs/day or near constant intrusion
2. INTERFERENCE DUE TO URGES/ THOUGHTS ABOUT SHOPPING How much do your urges/thoughts interfere with your social, work, or role functioning? Is there anything that you don't do because of them?	0 = None 1 = Mild, slight interference with social or occupational activity but overall performance not impaired. 2 = Moderate, definite interference with social or occupational performance, but still manageable. 3 = Severe, causes substantial impairment in social or occupational performance. 4 = Extreme, incapacitating.
3. DISTRESS ASSOCIATED WITH URGES/THOUGHTS ABOUT SHOPPING How much distress do your urges/thoughts about stealing cause you?	0 = None 1 = Mild, infrequent, and not too disturbing. 2 = Moderate, frequent, & disturbing, but still manageable. 3 = Severe, very frequent, and very disturbing. 4 = Extreme, near constant, and disabling distress.

4. RESISTANCE AGAINST URGES/ THOUGHTS OF SHOPPING How much of an effort do you make to resist these urges/thoughts? How often do you try to disregard or turn your attention away from these thoughts as they enter your mind?	0 = Makes effort to always resist, or symptoms so minimal that active resistance not needed. 1 = Tries to resist most of the time. 2 = Makes some effort to resist. 3 = Yields to all thoughts without attempting to control them, but does so with some resistance. 4 = Completely and willingly yields to all thoughts about shopping.
5. DEGREE OR CONTROL OVER URGES/THOUGHTS ABOUT SHOPPING How much control do you have over thoughts about shopping? How successful are you in stopping or diverting these thoughts? Can you dismiss them?	0 = Complete control. 1 = Much control, usually able to stop or divert thoughts with some effort and concentration. 2 = Moderate control, sometimes able to stop or divert thinking. 3 = Little control, rarely successful in stopping or dismissing thinking, can only divert attention with difficulty. 4 = No control, experience is completely involuntary, rarely able even momentarily to alter thoughts about shopping.
6. TIME SPENT IN ACTIVITIES RELATED TO SHOPPING How much time do you spend shopping? How much time do you spend compulsively shopping?	0 = None 1 = Mild, spends <1 h / day shopping 2 = Moderate, spends 1–3 h / day shopping. 3 = Severe, spends >3 and ≤8 h / day shopping. 4 = Extreme, spends >8 h / day shopping or near constant shopping episodes
7. INTERFERENCE DUE TO ACTIVITIES RELATED TO SHOPPING How much do the above activities interfere with you social, work, or role functioning? Is there anything that you don't do because of the shopping?	0 = None. 1 = Mild, slight interference with social or occupational activities, but overall performance not impaired. 2 = Moderate, definite interference with social or occupational performance, but still manageable. 3 = Severe, causes substantial impairment in social or occupational performance. 4 = Extreme, incapacitating.

8. DISTRESS ASSOCIATED WITH BEHAVIOR RELATED TO SHOPPING How would you feel if prevented from shopping? How anxious would you become?	0 = None. 1 = Mild, only slightly anxious if shopping prevented, or only slightly anxious 2 = Moderate, reports that anxiety would mount but remains manageable 3 = Severe, prominent, and very disturbing increase in anxiety if shopping interrupted. 4 = Extreme, incapacitating anxiety from any intervention aimed at modifying activity, or incapacitating anxiety develops during performance of shopping.
9. RESISTANCE AGAINST SHOPPING How much of an effort do you make to resist the compulsion?	0 = Makes an effort to always resist, or symptoms so minimal that active resistance not needed 1 = Tries to resist most of the time 2 = Makes some effort to resist. 3 = Yields to almost all compulsions without attempting to control them, but does so with some reluctance. 4 = Completely and willingly yields to almost all compulsions
10. DEGREE OF CONTROL OVER SHOPPING BEHAVIOR How strong is the drive to shop? How much control do you have over the compulsion?	0 = Complete control. 1 = Much control, experiences pressure to perform the behavior but usually able to exercise voluntary control over it. 2 = Moderate control, strong pressure to perform behavior, can control it only with difficulty. 3 = Little control, very strong drive to perform behavior, must be carried to completion, can only delay with difficulty. 4 = No control, drive to perform behavior experienced as completely involuntary and overpowering, rarely able even momentarily to delay activity.

Urge/Thought Subscale Score _____

Behavior Subscale Score _____

Total Score _____

Compulsive Buying Symptom Assessment Scale (CB-SAS)

The following questionnaire is aimed at evaluating your buying symptoms. Please **read** the questions **carefully** before you answer.

1) **If you had urges to buy during the past WEEK, on average, how strong were your urges to buy items? Circle the most appropriate number:**

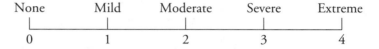

None	Mild	Moderate	Severe	Extreme
0	1	2	3	4

2) **During the past WEEK, how many times did you experience urges to buy items? Circle the most appropriate number.**

   0) None

   1) Once

   2) Two or three times

   3) Several to many times

   4) Constant or near constant

3) **During the past WEEK, how many hours (add up hours) were you preoccupied with your urges to buy? Circle the most appropriate number.**

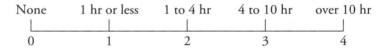

None	1 hr or less	1 to 4 hr	4 to 10 hr	over 10 hr
0	1	2	3	4

4) **During the past WEEK, how much were you able to control your urges? Circle the most appropriate number.**

Very much	Much	Moderate	Minimal	No control
0	1	2	3	4

5) During the past WEEK, how often did thoughts about shopping come up? Circle the most appropriate number.

0) None

1) Once

2) Two to four times

3) Several to many times

4) Constantly or nearly constantly

6) During the past WEEK, approximately how many hours (add up hours) did you spend thinking about shopping? Circle the most appropriate number.

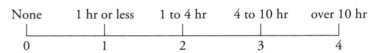

None	1 hr or less	1 to 4 hr	4 to 10 hr	over 10 hr
0	1	2	3	4

7) During the past WEEK, how much were you able to control your thoughts of buying? Circle the most appropriate number.

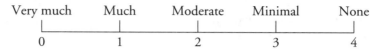

Very much	Much	Moderate	Minimal	None
0	1	2	3	4

8) During the past WEEK, on average, how much tension or excitement did you have <u>shortly before</u> you purchased an item? If you did not actually buy anything, please estimate how much anticipatory tension or excitement you believe you would have experienced, if you had purchased an item. Please circle the most appropriate number.

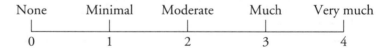

None	Minimal	Moderate	Much	Very much
0	1	2	3	4

9) During the past WEEK, on average, how much excitement and pleasure did you feel when you successfully bought an item? If you did not actually purchase anything, please estimate how much excitement and pleasure you believe you would have experienced if you had made a purchase. Circle the most appropriate number.

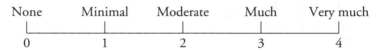

None	Minimal	Moderate	Much	Very much
0	1	2	3	4

10) During the past WEEK, how much emotional distress (mental pain or anguish, shame, guilt, embarrassment) has your buying caused you? Circle the most appropriate number.

None	Minimal	Moderate	Much	Very much
0	1	2	3	4

11) During the past WEEK, how much personal trouble (relationship, financial, legal, job, medical, or health) has your buying caused you? Circle the most appropriate number.

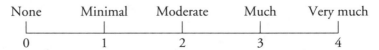

None	Minimal	Moderate	Much	Very much
0	1	2	3	4

NOTE TO INTERVIEWER: Use space below each question to describe responses to each question.

For each criterion, circle one of the following four choices:

? = Inadequate information

1 = absent or false

2 = subthreshold

3 = threshold or true

Criterion A. Have you ever set a fire on purpose?	**Deliberate and purposeful fire setting on more than one occasion.** <div align="right">?　1　2　3</div>
Criterion B. How were you feeling before you set the fire?	**Tension or affective arousal before the act.** <div align="right">?　1　2　3</div>
Criterion C. Are you fascinated by, or especially interested in, fires or things associated with fire?	**Fascination with, interest in, curiosity about, or attraction to fire and its situational contexts (e.g., paraphernalia, uses, consequences).** <div align="right">?　1　2　3</div>
Criterion D. How do you feel when you watch a fire?	**Intense pleasure, gratification, or relief when witnessing or participating in their aftermath.** <div align="right">?　1　2　3</div>

EXCLUSIONARY CRITERIA
(Criterion E., F., G.)

NOTE TO INTERVIEWER: If this module is being used in conjunction with the SCID, refer to Manic Episode or Conduct Disorder criteria.

(Circle "3" for fire setting behavior not better accounted for by the following criteria).

Criterion E.	The fire setting is not done for monetary gain, as an expression of sociopolitical ideology, to conceal criminal activity, to express anger or vengeance, or to improve one's living circumstances.
(rule out Antisocial Personality Disorder or Conduct Disorder).	
Why have you set fires?	
If this module is being used in conjunction with the SCID-II, refer to Antisocial Personality Disorder Criteria. If Antisocial Personality Disorder criteria are not met, you may rate as "fire setting behavior not better accounted for by antisocial personality disorder."	?　1　2　3
If Antisocial Personality Disorder criteria not asked, Before you were 15 years old, did you … initiate physical fights? … bully others? … use weapons? … act physically cruel to others? … act physically cruel to animals? … force someone into sexual activity? … set fires? … deliberately destroy property? … break into someone else's car or home? … run away from home or stay out all night?	
Criterion F.	The fire setting is not done in response to a delusion or hallucination.
I'd like to ask you about unusual experiences…	?　1　2　3
Have you ever set fires because you felt that a person was going out of their way to hurt you or give you a hard time?	
Have you set fires because you felt you were especially important in some way, or had special powers?	
Have you set fires because someone or something outside yourself was controlling your actions against your will?	
Have you set fires because you heard voices of people telling you to set fires, even when no one was with you?	
(If yes): Is this the reason (use subject's reason) that you *usually* set fires?	

Criterion G. Had you been drinking or using substances before setting a fire?	The fire setting is not a result of impaired judgment (e.g., Substance Intoxication). ? 1 2 3

To meet diagnostic criteria for pyromania, the subject must meet threshold for all criteria, and must not meet exclusionary (Criterion E, F, G) criteria.

Final determination for diagnosis of Pyromania:

Present		Absent

The following questions are aimed at evaluating pyromania symptoms. Please **read** the questions **carefully** before you answer.

1) **If you had urges to set a fire during the past WEEK, on average, how strong were your urges? Please circle the most appropriate number:**

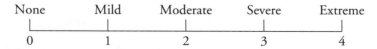

None	Mild	Moderate	Severe	Extreme
0	1	2	3	4

2) **During the past WEEK, how many times did you experience urges to set fires? Please circle the most appropriate number.**

   0) None

   1) Once

   2) Two to four times

   3) Several to many times

   4) Constantly or nearly constantly

3) **During the past WEEK, how many hours (add up hours) were you preoccupied with your urges to set fires? Please circle the most appropriate number.**

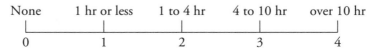

None	1 hr or less	1 to 4 hr	4 to 10 hr	over 10 hr
0	1	2	3	4

4) **During the past WEEK, how much were you able to control your urges? Please circle the most appropriate number.**

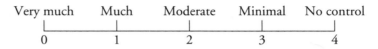

Very much	Much	Moderate	Minimal	No control
0	1	2	3	4

5) **During the past WEEK, how often did thoughts about setting fires come up? Please circle the most appropriate number.**

0) None

1) Once

2) Two to four times

3) Several to many times

4) Constantly or nearly constantly

6) **During the past WEEK, approximately how many hours (add up hours) did you spend thinking about setting fires? Please circle the most appropriate number.**

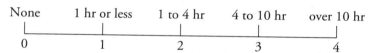

None	1 hr or less	1 to 4 hr	4 to 10 hr	over 10 hr
0	1	2	3	4

7) During the past WEEK, how much were you able to control your thoughts of setting fires? Please circle the most appropriate number.

Very much	Much	Moderate	Minimal	None
0	1	2	3	4

8) During the past WEEK, on average, how much tension or excitement did you have <u>shortly before</u> you set a fire? If you did not actually set a fire, please estimate how much anticipatory tension or excitement you believe you would have experienced, if you had set a fire. Please circle the most appropriate number.

None	Minimal	Moderate	Much	Very much
0	1	2	3	4

9) During the past WEEK, on average, how much excitement and pleasure did you feel when you successfully set a fire? If you did not actually set a fire, please estimate how much excitement and pleasure you believe you would have experienced if you had set a fire. Please circle the most appropriate number.

None	Minimal	Moderate	Much	Very much
0	1	2	3	4

10) During the past WEEK, how much emotional distress (mental pain or anguish, shame, guilt, embarrassment) has your fire setting caused you? Circle the most appropriate number.

None	Minimal	Moderate	Much	Very much
0	1	2	3	4

11) During the past WEEK, how much personal trouble (relationship, financial, legal, job, medical or health) has your fire setting caused you? Please circle the most appropriate number.

None	Minimal	Moderate	Much	Very much
0	1	2	3	4

The Consequences of the Impulse Control Problem

1. **At present, to what extent does your impulse control problem affect your <u>social life</u> (reduction of the number of friends, isolation, abandoning social activities, etc.)?**

Read all the choices

0	1	2	3	4	5	NA
Not at all No problem	Very little	Somewhat	Moderately	Much	A great deal Severe problems	

Explain:

_____

_____

_____

_____

_____

2. **At present, to what extent does your impulse control problem behavior affect your <u>marital life</u> (arguments, decrease in time spent with partner, irritability, frequency of sexual activities, etc.)**

Read all the choices

0	1	2	3	4	5	NA
Not at all No problem	Very little	Somewhat	Moderately	Much	A great deal Severe problems	

Explain:

_____

_____

_____

_____

_____

3. **At present, to what extent does your impulse control problem affect your <u>family life</u> (absences, decrease in time spent with children, irritability, etc.)?**

Read all the choices

0	1	2	3	4	5	NA
Not at all No problem	Very little	Somewhat	Moderately	Much	A great deal Severe problems	

Explain:

_____

_____

_____

_____

4. **At present, to what extent does your impulse control problem affect your <u>work</u> (decrease in efficiency, absences, lateness, lack of concentration, etc.)?**

Read all the choices

0	1	2	3	4	5	NA
Not at all No problem	Very little	Somewhat	Moderately	Much	A great deal Severe problems	

Explain:

_____

_____

_____

_____

5. **At present, to what extent does your impulse control problem affect your <u>mood</u> (anxiety, worries, stress, depression, etc.)?**

Read all the choices

0	1	2	3	4	5	NA
Not at all No problem	Very little	Somewhat	Moderately	Much	A great deal Severe problems	

Explain:

_____

_____

_____

_____

6. **At present, to what extent does your impulse control problem affect your <u>sleep</u> (difficulty falling asleep or staying asleep, waking up too early in the morning, etc.)?**

Read all the choices

0	1	2	3	4	5	NA
Not at all No problem	Very little	Somewhat	Moderately	Much	A great deal Severe problems	

Explain:

_____

_____

_____

_____

7. **At present, to what extent does your impulse control problem affect your <u>physical health</u> (weight loss, stomach ulcers, headaches, etc.)?**

Read all the choices

0	1	2	3	4	5	NA
Not at all No problem	Very little	Somewhat	Moderately	Much	A great deal Severe problems	

Explain:

_____

_____

_____

_____

8. **At present, to what extent does your impulse control problem affect your <u>financial situation</u> (**Go to question #9 if the problem has no effect on finances**)?**

Read all the choices

0	1	2	3	4	5	NA
Not at all No problem	Very little	Somewhat	Moderately	Much	A great deal Severe problems	

Explain:

_____

_____

_____

_____

8a. Have you ever declared bankruptcy?

        YES   NO

If yes, when? _____ *(indicate the year)*

What was the amount of the debt? $_____

What amount was directly related to gambling/buying? $_____

8b. At present, do you have gambling/buying debts?

        YES   NO

    If yes, to whom do you owe money?

        Bank/Credit Union   ___   Amount owed $_____

        Partner   ___   Amount owed $_____

        Relative   ___   Amount owed $_____

        Friend   ___   Amount owed $_____

Colleague	___	Amount owed $_____
Loan shark	___	Amount owed $_____
Other	___	Amount owed $_____

8c. What do you estimate is the total amount of money lost as a result of gambling up to today? If CB is the primary problem, how much would you estimate you have spent to date as a result of your CB habit?

_____ $

9. At present, to what extent does your impulse control problem affect your <u>quality of life</u> (housing, diet, purchases of personal possession, personal care, etc.)?

Read all the choices

0	1	2	3	4	5	NA
Not at all No problem	Very little	Somewhat	Moderately	Much	A great deal Severe problems	

Explain:

_____
_____
_____
_____

9a. What legal consequences have you experienced as a result of your impulse control problem? For example: arrests, time served, fined, probation, etc.

Explain:

_____
_____
_____
_____
_____
_____
_____
_____
_____

1. In the past 12 months, have you ever SERIOUSLY thought about committing suicide (putting an end to your life)?

    YES   NO

1b. If YES, had you thought about a way to do it?

    YES   NO

1c. Was this thought mainly linked to your impulse control problem?

    YES   NO

1d. Have you attempted suicide (tried to end your life) in the last 12 months?

    YES   NO

2. Have you ever attempted suicide?

    YES   NO

2b. IF YES, in what year? _____

2c. Explain the context:

    _____
    _____
    _____
    _____

3. Are you presently considering suicide?

    YES   NO

Comments:

    _____
    _____
    _____
    _____
    _____
    _____

References

American Psychiatric Association. (2000). *Diagnostic and statistical manual of mental disorders* (Revised 4th ed.). Washington, DC: American Psychiatric Publishing, Inc.

Black, D. W., Repertinger, S., Gaffney, G. R., & Gabel, J. (1998). Family history and psychiatric comorbidity in persons with compulsive buying: Preliminary findings. *American Journal of Psychiatry, 155*(7), 960–963.

Carter, B. L., & Tiffany, S. T. (1999). Meta-analysis of cue-reactivity in addiction research. *Addiction, 94*(3), 327–340.

Crockford, D. N., & el-Guebaly, N. (1998). Psychiatric comorbidity in pathological gambling: A critical review. *Canadian Journal of Psychiatry, 43*(1), 43–50.

DiClemente, C. C. & Hughes, S. O. (1990). Stages of change profiles in alcoholism treatment. *Journal of Substance Abuse, 2,* 217–235.

Dimidjian, S., Martell, C. R., Addis, M. E., & Herman-Dunn, R. (2008). Behavioral activation for depression, in D.H. Barlow, *Clinical handbook of psychological disorders : A step by step treatment manual (4th Edition).* (pp. *328–364*). New York: The Guilford Press.

Echeburúa, E., Báez, C., & Fernández-Montalvo, J. (1996). Comparaive effectiveness of three therapeutic modalities in psychological treatment of pathological gambling. *Behavioral and Cognitive Psychotherapy, 24,* 51–72.

Foa, E. B., & Kozak, M. J. (1986). Emotional processing of fear: Exposure to corrective information. *Psychological Bulletin, 99*(1), 20–35.

Frost, R. O., Kim, H. J., Morris, C., Bloss, C., Murry-Close, M., & Steketee, G. (1998). Hoarding, compulsive buying and reasons for saving. *Behavioral Research and Therapy, 36*(7–8), 657–664.

Grant, J. E. (2006). Understanding and treating kleptomania: new models and new treatments. *The Israel Journal of Psychiatry and Related Sciences, 43*(2), 81–87.

Grant, J. E. (2008). *Impulse control disorders: A clinician's guide to understanding and treating behavioral addictions.* New York: W. W. Norton & Company.

Grant J. E., & Kim, S.W. (2002a). Clinical characteristics and associated psychopathology of 22 patients with kleptomania. *Comprehensive Psychiatry, 43*(5), 378–384.

Grant J. E., & Kim, S.W. (2002b). An open label study of naltrexone in the treatment of kleptomania. *Journal of Clinical Psychiatry, 63,* 349–356.

Grant, J. E., & Kim, S. W. (2003). *Stop me because I can't stop myself: Taking control of impulsive behavior.* New York: McGraw-Hill.

Grant, J. E., & Potenza, M. N. (2006). Compulsive aspects of impulse control disorders. *Psychiatric Clinics of North America, 29*(2), 539–551.

Grant J. E., & Kim, S. W. (2007). Clinical characteristics and psychiatric comorbidity of pyromania. *Journal of Clinical Psychiatry, 68*(11), 1717–1722.

Grant, J. E., Brewer, J. A., & Potenza, M. N. (2006). The neurobiology of substance and behavioral addictions. *CNS Spectrums, 11*(12), 924–930.

Grant, J. E., Kim, S. W., & McCabe, J. S. (2006). A Structured Clinical Interview for Kleptomania (SCI-K): preliminary validity and reliability testing. *International Journal of Methods in Psychiatric Research, 15*(2), 83–94.

Grant, J. E., Kim, S. W., & Odlaug, B. L. (2009). A double-blind, placebo-controlled study of opiate antagonist, naltrexone, in the treatment of kleptomania. *Biological Psychiatry, 65*(7), 600–606.

Grant, J. E., Steinberg, M. A., Kim, S. W., Rounsaville, B. J., & Potenza, M. N. (2004). Preliminary validity and reliability testing of a structured clinical interview for pathological gambling (SCI-PG). *Psychiatry Research, 128,* 79–88.

Grant, J. E., Levine, L., Kim, D., & Potenza, M. N. (2005). Impulse control disorders in adult psychiatric inpatients. *American Journal of Psychiatry, 162*(11), 2184–2188.

Grant, J. E., Donahue, C., Odlaug, B. L., Kim, S. W., Miller, M. J., & Petry, N. M. (2009). Imaginal desensitization plus motivational interviewing in the treatment of pathological gambling: A randomized controlled trial. *British Journal of Psychiatry, 195*(3), 266–267.

Holden, C. (2001). 'Behavioral' addictions: do they exist? *Science, 294*(5544), 980–982.

Kim, S. W., Grant, J. E., Potenza, M. N., Blanco, C., & Hollander, E. (2009). The Gambling Symptom Assessment Scale (G-SAS): a reliability and validity study. *Psychiatry Research, 166,* 76–84.

Koran, L. M., Aboujaoude, E. N., & Gamel, N. N. (2007). Escitalopram treatment of kleptomania: An open-label trial followed by double-blind discontinuation. *Journal of Clinical Psychiatry, 68,* 422–427.

Kushner, M. G., Abrams, K., Donahue, C. B., Thuras, P., Frost, R., & Kim, S. W. (2007). Urge to gamble in problem gamblers exposed to a casino environment. *Journal of Gambling Studies, 23*(2), 121–132.

Ladouceur, R., & Lachance, S. (2007). *Overcoming pathological gambling: therapist guide.* Oxford, UK: Oxford University Press.

Ladouceur, R., & Lachance, S. (2007). *Overcoming pathological gambling: workbook.* Oxford, UK: Oxford University Press.

Lejoyeux, M., Arbaretaz, M., McLoughlin, M., & Adès, J. (2002). Impulse control disorders and depression. *The Journal of Nervous and Mental Disease, 190*(5), 310–314.

McElroy, S. L., Keck, P. E., Pope, H. G, Smith, J. M., & Strakowski, S. M. (1994). Compulsive buying: A report of 20 cases. *Journal of Clinical Psychiatry, 55*(6), 242–248.

McElroy, S.L., Pope, H.G., Hudson, J.I., Keck, P.E., Jr., & White, K.L. (1991). Kleptomania: A report of 20 cases. *American Journal of Psychiatry, 148*(5), 652–657.

McNeilly, D. P., & Burke, W. J. (1998). Stealing lately: a case of late-onset kleptomania. *International Journal of Geriatric Psychiatry, 13*(2), 116–121.

Miller, W. R., & Rollnick, S. (2002). *Motivational interviewing: Preparing people for change.* New York: The Guilford Press.

Miltenberger, R. G., Redlin, J., Crosby, R., Stickney, M., Mitchell, J., Wonderlich, S., Smith, J. (2003). Direct and retrospective assessment of factors contributing to compulsive buying. *Journal of Behavior Therapy and Experimental Psychiatry, 34*(1), 1–9.

Monehan, P. W., Black, D. W., & Gabel, J. (1996). Reliability and validity of a scale to measure change in a persons compulsive buying. *Psychiatry Research, 64*(1), 59–67.

Najavits, L. M. (2003). How to design an effective treatment outcome study. *Journal of Gambling Studies, 19*(3), 317–337.

National Gambling Impact Study Commission. (1999). *National Gambling Impact Study Commission Final Report.* Washington, D.C.

Odlaug, B. L., & Grant, J. E. (2010). Impulse-control disorders in a college sample: results from the self-administered Minnesota impulse disorders interview (MIDI). *Primary Care Companion to the Journal of Clinical Psychiatry, 12*(2), e1–e5.

Pallanti, S., DeCaria, C. M., Grant, J. E., Urpe, M., & Hollander, E. (2005). Reliability and validity of the pathological gambling adaptation of the Yale-Brown Obsessive-Compulsive Scale (PG-YBOCS). *Journal of Gambling Studies, 21*(4), 431–443.

Petry, N. M. (2005). Gamblers anonymous and cognitive-behavioral therapies for pathological gamblers. *Journal of Gambling Studies, 21*(1), 27–33.

Petry, N. M., Ammerman, Y., Bohl, J., Doersch, A., Gay, H., Kadden, R., Molina, C., Steinberg, K. (2006). Cognitive-behavioral therapy for pathological gamblers. *Journal of Consulting and Clinical Psychology, 74*(3), 555–567.

Phelan, J. (2002). Childhood kleptomania: Two clinical case studies with implications for further research. *Psychology and Education – An Interdisciplinary Journal, 39*(3–4), 19–21.

Sodano, R., Wulfert, E. (2010). Cue reactivity in active pathological, abstinent pathological, and regular gamblers. *Journal of Gambling Studies, 26*(1), 53–65.

Sylvain, C., Ladouceur, R., & Boisvert, J. (1997). Cognitive and behavioral treatment of pathological gambling: A controlled study. *Journal of Consulting & Clinical Psychology, 65*(5), 727–732.

Symes, R. A., & Nicki, R. M. (1997). A preliminary consideration of cue-exposure, response prevention treatment for pathological gambling behaviour: Two case studies. *Journal of Gambling Studies, 13*(2), 145–157.

Toneatto, T., & Ladouceur, R. (2003). Treatment of pathological gambling: A critical review of the literature. *Psychology of Addictive Behaviors, 17*(4), 284–292.

Suggested Readings

We owe a great deal of thanks to those clinicians and researchers who have published works on the conditions described throughout this manual. Those interested in reading more about impulse control disorders may wish to read the some of the following text. This list is not exhaustive nor is it inclusive of all of the fine work published over the years. We merely list these as a starting point for those interested in reading more about these conditions.

Aboujaoude, E., & Koran, L. M. (editors) (2010). *Impulse control disorders.* Cambridge, UK: Cambridge University Press.

Black, D. W., Repertinger, S., Gaffney, G. R., & Gabel, J. (1998). Family History and psychiatric comorbidity in persons with compulsive buying: Preliminary findings. *American Journal of Psychiatry, 155*(7), 960–963.

Grant, J. E. *Impulse control disorders: A clinician's guide to understanding and treating behavioral addictions.* New York: W.W. Norton & Company.

Grant, J. E., Donahue, C., Odlaug, B. L., Kim, S. W., Miller, M. J., & Petry, N. M. (2009). Imaginal desensitization plus motivational interviewing in the treatment of pathological gambling: A randomized controlled trial. *British Journal of Psychiatry 195*(3), 266–267.

Grant J. E., & Potenza, M. N., (editors). (in press). *Oxford library of psychology: Oxford handbook of impulse control disorders.* Oxford, UK: Oxford University Press.

Hollander, E., & Stein, D. J. (editors). (2005). *Clinical manual of impulse-control disorders.* New York: American Psychiatric Publishing, Inc.

Ladouceur, R., & Lachance, S. (2007). *Overcoming pathological gambling: workbook.* Oxford, UK: Oxford University Press.

Ladouceur, R., Sylvain, C., Boutin, C., Lachance, S., Doucet, C., Leblond, J., et al. (2001). Cognitive treatment of pathological gambling. *Journal of Nervous and Mental Disorders, 189,* 766–773.

Miller, W. R., & Rollnick, S. (2002). *Motivational interviewing: Preparing people for change.* New York: The Guilford Press.

Mitchell, J. E., Burgard, M., Faber, R., Crosby, R D., & de Zwaan M. (2006). Cognitive behavioral therapy for compulsive buying disorder. *Behaviour Research and Therapy, 44*(12), 1859–1865.

Petry, N. M. (2004). *Pathological gambling: Etiology, comorbidity, and treatment.* Washington, D.C., American Psychological Association.

About the Authors

Jon E. Grant, JD, MD, MPH, is a Professor of Psychiatry and Director of the Impulsive Compulsive Disorders Clinic at the University of Minnesota Medical School. An author of over 200 peer-reviewed scientific publications, Dr. Grant serves on the editorial boards of several journals and is the Editor in Chief of the *Journal of Gambling Studies.*

Christopher B. Donahue, PhD, is an Assistant Professor in the Department of Psychiatry at the University of Minnesota, Minneapolis, MN. He is involved in ongoing collaboration with coauthors investigating treatments for impulse control disorders. Dr. Donahue has published book chapters and refereed journal articles on the treatment of anxiety and impulse control disorders. Other areas of research include cognitive-behavioral therapy for comorbid alcohol and anxiety disorders, and exposure/response prevention treatment of obsessive-compulsive disorder. Dr. Donahue divides his time between research and an independent clinical practice.

Brian L. Odlaug, BA, is a graduate student in the School of Public Health at the University of Minnesota, and concurrently works in the Department of Psychiatry as the Lead Clinical Research Coordinator for the Impulse Control Disorders Clinic. He has published over 50 peer-reviewed articles and book chapters exploring the phenomenology, treatment, and clinical characteristics of impulse control disorders and other psychiatric conditions. His current research interests include examining the public health consequences of behavioral addictions on individual quality of life, and their economic and social impact in the general population.